BORDER CONTROL

ENTRANCE EXAM

UTTERLY UNOFFICIAL AND UNSANCTIONED

BORDER CONTROL

ENTRANCE EXAM

ARE YOU BRITISH ENOUGH FOR POST-BREXIT BRITAIN?

CONTENTS

INTRODUCTION

Who could have imagined that a petty internal beef within the gammon fringes of the Conservative Party would divide the nation, tear the United Kingdom away from the European Union and trigger possibly the biggest constitutional crisis since Danny Dyer appeared on *Who Do You Think You Are?*

With hyperbole and naked self-interest poisoning both sides of the argument within the media and our venal ruling class, it will be another five hundred years before ordinary people can declare Brexit a triumphant second Dunkirk or a squib so damp that half the population will literally drown to death.

Only one thing is certain: this book will never lie to you or seek to profit from your wilful ignorance. This patriotic home testing kit (despite technically being printed in the EU) can accurately measure whether you are British enough to survive in Little England after we finally sever ties with Brussels or whether you should buy a stone cottage in the Pyrenees.

Now we stand at an historic moment, as we courageously prepare, with pluck and calm assurance, to meander together into an interminable transitional period. Deep knowledge about the weather, queuing, going for a curry or chasing a truckle of cheese down a hill in Gloucestershire, are just some of the varied and totally non-parochial credentials that will hastily establish your indigenous Britishness, whilst our 'post-brexit _____land' (insert the word 'waste', 'wonder' or 'pound' depending on your IQ and political literacy) looms over the horizon.

TEST No. 274680 · Time limit 5 minutes

FISH AND CHIPS

Is there anything more post-Brexit British than fish and chips, apart from chicken tikka masala? Fried fish was first introduced by Sephardic Jews settling in England in the seventeenth century, although it was another two hundred years before it was paired with fried chipped potatoes, an early example of fusion cookery. Debate rages as to whether the North or South serves the best fish supper. Quality varies greatly throughout the nation because most Brits will tolerate any old deep-fried cack without realising they could do so much better. An added bonus of a visit to 'the chippy' is that it often involves queuing, another thing Brits love to do.

1. In 1896, Sam Isaacs opened the first *what* in Whitechapel, London?

   a. spam email

   b. malt vinegar factory

   c. sit-down fish and chip restaurant

   d. jar of pickled eggs

2. Where's the best place to eat fish and chips?

   a. on the seafront

   b. in the car

   c. at home in bed watching *Ant and Dec's Saturday Night Takeaway*

   d. any of the above

3. What's the most important constituent of the perfect fish and chips?

a. The frying medium is key: traditionally beef dripping or lard.

b. Fresh vegetable oil; it's both healthy and tasty.

c. succulent white cod or haddock flakes in a crispy orange batter, thick golden chips, fried to order

d. Who cares? In common with most clueless Brits, serve me soggy chips and a greasy slab of grey pollock, and I'll shovel it gratefully into my drunken face like a consumptive vagrant.

4. Name three things that you would expect to see in a fish and chip shop that everyone hates.

a. pickled eggs

b. acne

c. jar of cocks

d. flimsy wooden fork

5. **What's the difference between a saveloy and a jumbo sausage?**

a. about twenty pence

b. A saveloy is usually bright red and normally boiled.

c. A saveloy is traditionally made from pig brains; a sausage is made with everything else.

d. all of the above

6. **How do you dispose of the paper and polystyrene containers after eating your meal?**

a. Put them in a rubbish bin or take them home.

b. Put them in a recycling bin.

c. Put them on the floor adjacent to an overflowing public rubbish bin.

d. Drive twenty miles from the urban slum where I live into the countryside in my tastelessly pimped Vauxhall Corsa with four of my mates, and dump the litter in a hedge or force feed it to a horse.

7. **Introduced in 1966, the Maris Piper potato was one of the first potato varieties bred to be resistant to what?**

a. frost

b. the potato cyst nematode, *Globodera rostochiensis*

c. fire

d. bovine spongiform encephalopathy (BSE)

8. **How are mushy peas made?**

a. They squash regular peas and leave them on a windowsill

b. Errant peas are swept up from the floors of canning factories and soaked in Benzedrine.

c. Chickpeas pass through the bile duct of a civet cat.

d. Marrowfat peas are soaked in water and sodium bicarbonate.

9. **During the Second World War, which prominent British figure referred to fish and chips as 'good companions'?**

a. J B Priestley

b. Vera Lynn

c. Winston Churchill

d. Queen Elizabeth II

10. **There are 1,200 McDonald's and about 9,000 Indian restaurants in the UK. Approximately how many fish and chip shops are there?**

a. 6,400

b. 3,700

c. 21,600

d. 10,500

TEST No. 274681 • Time limit 2 minutes

OWNING A DOG

The UK is a nation of dog lovers. Groucho Marx famously remarked: 'Outside of a dog, a book is a man's best friend. Inside of a dog it's too dark to read'. That's sound advice for any book-loving dog lover, but isn't much help if you want to spend two minutes choosing the dog that's right for you. So here's a handy guide for any wannabe Brit looking for the ultimate Christmas present or to find something that will destroy your lawn and love you unconditionally.

Begin here and follow the arrows.

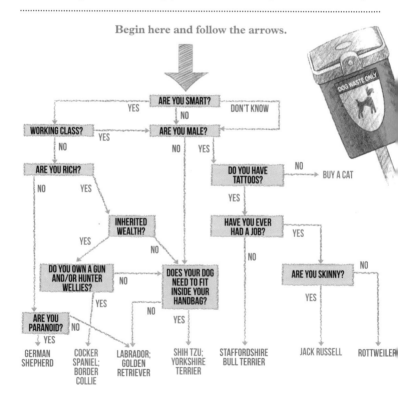

THE RULES OF CRICKET

Cricket is a bat-and-ball game played between two teams, each of eleven players, in a field, at the centre of which is a rectangular 20-metre 'pitch' with a wicket at each end comprising three wooden sticks called stumps. The winning team is the one that scores the most runs, with the added jeopardy that a match may drag on for five days only to be declared a dead heat because of rain. Few other sports can rival this absurd amount of potentially meaningless effort.

The origins of cricket are uncertain, but it probably arose in south-east England in the middle of the sixteenth century and then spread around the world. It's accurate to say that it's one of the many sports invented by the British, which today regularly delivers a humiliating defeat for its progenitor nation.

Cricket is terminally boring and follows the Law of Viridescence, the generally acknowledged principle that the buttock-clenching tedium of a sport is directly proportionate to the amount of playing area that is coloured green. Cricket is usually played on an area of grass of more than $17,000m^2$ (although officially there are no fixed dimensions so there is no theoretical limit to just how dreary cricket can be, which is why players habitually tamper with their balls).

YOUR THREE-MINUTE CHALLENGE

You have three minutes to correctly name each fielding position (red dot) on the field for a right-handed batsman. Choose from the list below, but watch out, as ten of the names are red herrings that belong on an EU fishing quota.

Long stop	Silly mid-on	No point	Fifth column	Wicket keeper
Straight hit	Mid-on	Complete twat	Hard-on	Long off
Third leg	Mid-off	Square leg	Semi	Long on
Point	Slip	Silly leg	Fine leg	Gully
Cover	Long leg	Third man	Open leg	Fly slip
Deep	Deep backward	Coarse leg	Straight	Open fly

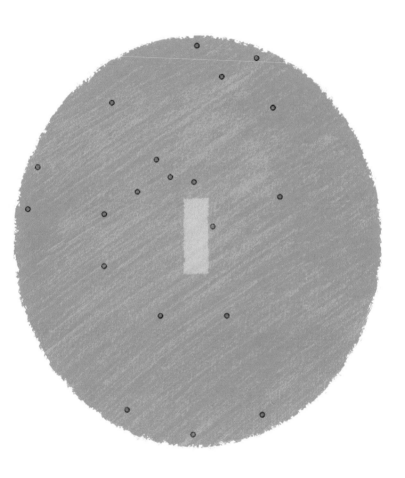

TEST No. 274682 • Time limit 10 minutes

THE SUNDAY ROAST

Nothing can beat the traditional British roast dinner. Even if you visit the most depressingly generic super chain pub, it can usually manage to produce an edible carvery, but the homemade family Sunday roast is only topped in the national psyche by a bacon sandwich (in a recent poll conducted by T-Mobile, the top five things Brits loved best about their country were bacon sandwiches, roast dinners, cups of tea, British history and the BBC, although 'Sunday lunch' also came in at number 16, just one below The Queen).

There are fifty Sunday roast-related words hidden in the word search opposite. See if you can find them all, and then sit in front of the telly and have a snooze.

bacon	herbs	roasters
baking tray	horseradish	rosemary
beef	juices	sage and onion
boiled	lamb	sausages
breast	leeks	silverside
broccoli	leg	spring greens
butternut squash	mint	sprouts
cabbage	moist	stuffing
carrot	mustard	swede
carving	parsnip	tender
cauliflower	Parson's Nose	topside
chicken	peas	trimmings
colander	pigs in blankets	turkey
crackling	pork	vegetables
crisp	potatoes	wishbone
garlic	rib	Yorkshire pudding
gravy	roasted	

```
T R I M M I N G S E D I S P O T U R K E Y H F
W A E I V V L K R O P W W V E G E T A B L E S
I U C P V G N I D D U P E R I H S K R O Y C M
S U G Y H K Q D Q L D K D V K I N T G Y L R U
H I P Y G T S I O M B B E P A R S N I P J I S
B J U I C E S G S H M A Q Y V I I M Z Y D S T
O R I L O C C O R B O K C O R V F Y M A H P A
N R E Y C Z Q N X Y A I C A R R O T V U W L R
E O W A B A X S K Z M N Y A S T U F F I N G D
Y S N N S E B S N G K G C L E G H W F B B X F
C E S T P T E B B U T T E R N U T S Q U A S H
H M R E X E P F A O P R R Q E X G H Y O V B S
I A E N J V A H U G U A S E O T A T O P O H C
C R T D C F E S B D E Y L Q W R I B Y I M R R
K Y S E J R F O B Y V A R G L O P D L F S O A
E X A R B J S I L V E R S I D E L E W J E A C
N G O S P R I N G G R E E N S G D F W M G S K
P A R S O N S N O S E L J D T S N Z I T A T L
P I G S I N B L A N K E T S N O K V M L S E I
S P R O U T S G U R B M A L C A M E J Y U D N
S X M C I L R A G K D P W A E I L A E Q A A G
H O R S E R A D I S H B B I N C C O R L S S C
S A G E A N D O N I O N M T A X X B C O T G R
```

15

LAST NIGHT OF THE PROMS

The Proms, more formally known as the Henry Wood Promenade Concerts, broadcasted by the BBC, is an annual eight-week summer programme of orchestral classical music concerts, held mostly in the Royal Albert Hall in London. The last night is like the end of term at boarding school – there's a party atmosphere and you have to pay through the nose to take part because the majority of tickets are allocated to those who have already attended at least five other Proms concerts during that season. So much for benign populism.

A mere 200 tickets are reserved for the plebs (mainly upper-middle-class music students) in an open ballot or, they can queue for standing room tickets on the day (the queues round the block come second only to Wimbledon). Alternatively, anyone can attend one of the Proms in the Park events (there's one in Hyde Park and in several other major cities) and watch live on a big screen video link-up.

The Last Night concert usually consists of a first half of popular classics with a second half of British patriotic stuff, including Edward Elgar's 'Pomp & Circumstance March No. 1' (Land of Hope and Glory), Henry Wood's 'Fantasia on British Sea Songs' and Thomas Arne's 'Rule, Britannia!'. The concert concludes with Hubert Parry's 'Jerusalem', the British national anthem and much waving of Union Flags. It's a great tradition that will show Johnny Foreigner that a few Brits still have money to burn and can afford to let their hair down post-Brexit.

YOUR THREE-MINUTE CHALLENGE

You have three minutes to answer the five questions below.

1. Until Queen Victoria laid the foundation stone in 1867, The Royal Albert Hall was originally supposed to have been called:

   a. the New London Coliseum

   b. the Central Hall of Arts and Sciences

   c. the South Kensington Concert Hall

   d. the Queen Victoria Auditorium.

2. What is a tessitura?

   a. comfortable humidity for musical instruments

   b. comfortable shoes

   c. comfortable pair of red corduroy trousers

   d. comfortable vocal range

3. The words from 'Jerusalem' were taken from a poem by William Blake, inspired by which Somerset-based apocryphal story?

   a. Jesus and Joseph of Arimathea travel to England and visit Glastonbury.

   b. John the Baptist visits the Roman baths at *Aquae Sulis* (Bath).

   c. The twelve apostles spend a bank holiday weekend at Brean Leisure Park, near Burnham-on-Sea.

   d. Mary Magdalene purchases a 'holy lamb' from the farmers' market at the 'Ancient Royal Town of Wessex' (Somerton).

4. If the flagpole is on the left-hand side, which is the correct way to fly the Union Flag?

   (a)　　　　(b)

5. Which of the following are permitted at the Last Night concert?

   a. fancy dress

   b. party poppers

   c. balloons

   d. patriotic t-shirts

TEST No. 274683 • Time limit 4 minutes

DRIVING IN BRITAIN

Motoring's tough and it's getting tougher. The roads are full of idiots who are out to get you, and that's just the cyclists; the lunatics in their cars are even worse. They'll slow you down, cut you up, they'll overtake and they'll destroy your no-claims bonus. One of the main reasons everyone in the country is such a rubbish driver is that no one knows what the signs mean. Can you match these twenty signs with their alternative interpretation?

Beware Nazi road painters

Man struggling with umbrella

Prostate exam

Stunt motorcyclists

Red cars keep to the left

Alien abductions

Dumb lorry drivers

Cut-and-shut job

Sandy camel toe

Tailgating BMW drivers

Beeyooobs
Beware rickets!
Ferry service cancelled
Giant electronic piano mat
No admission without a tie

Ip Man
Suitable for home freezing
Juggling workshop
Road buffering ahead
Crucifixion

Technical Challenge #3 • Time limit 5 minutes

THE FULL ENGLISH BREAKFAST

The full English breakfast includes bacon, sausages, eggs, fried bread, toast, mushrooms, cooked plum tomatoes, optional black pudding, baked beans, hash browns and a hot beverage such as coffee or tea. It's a far superior start to the day to the derisory snack on offer in the rest of Europe, commonly referred to as the continental breakfast, which usually consists of bread or pastries, fruit juice, jam and possibly a few measly slices of cured meat. No wonder mainland Europeans have to lie down in the afternoon. The Battle of Waterloo may have been fought on rations of bread and salt beef, but thankfully the Victorians didn't skimp on the first meal of the day, otherwise we'd never have won two world wars.

MAGIC SQUARE BREAKFAST

A tin of beans contains half a gram of fat.

A rasher of bacon contains one more gram of fat than a fried egg.

Each row, column and diagonal adds up to the fat contents of two sausages.

How many grams of fat each are there in a rasher of bacon, a sausage and a fried egg?

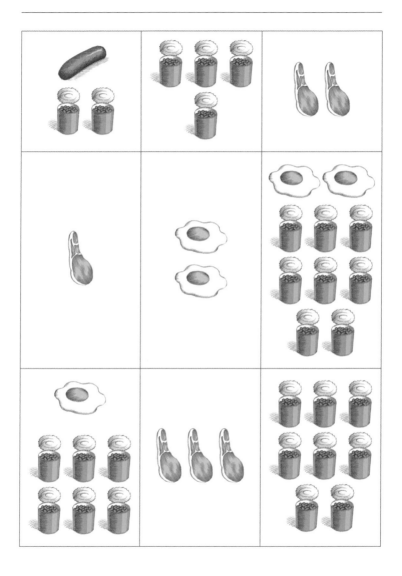

TEST No. 274684 • Time limit 5 minutes

NATIONAL STEPHENS

Why is it that so many of our national treasures are called Stephen? Or maybe it seems that way because it's easy to name at least two without hesitation. Anyway, national Stephens are celebrities – usually sports people or entertainers, with the occasional academic – who have so endeared themselves in the country's psyche that life just wouldn't be the same without them. To qualify as a national Stephen, you probably have to be at least middle aged, have mass appeal, have fooled the British public into thinking that you are fleetingly capable of being self-deprecating and enjoy almost saturation media coverage without losing your rag or your bankability. How well do you know our National Stephens? In each question, you must spot the one sentence that was not uttered by the National Stephen in question.

1. Stephen Fry

a. I've always had great respect for Paddington because he is amusingly English and eccentric.

b. Education is an admirable thing, but it is well to remember from time-to-time that nothing that is worth knowing can be taught.

c. My vocal cords are made of tweed. I give off an air of Oxford donnishness and old BBC wirelesses.

d. Books are no more threatened by Kindle than stairs by elevators.

2. Stephen Hawking

a. I deal in tough mathematical questions every day, but please don't ask me to help with Brexit.

b. Every carbon atom in every living thing on the planet was produced in the heart of a dying star.

c. It would not be beyond the realms of possibility that somewhere outside of our own universe lies another different universe. And in that universe Zayn is still in One Direction.

d. Not only does God definitely play dice, but He sometimes confuses us by throwing them where they can't be seen.

3. Stephen Frears

a. In my house I'm the boss, my wife is just the decision maker.

b. It's all been a wonderful accident. I'm still amazed every time I finish a film.

c. I have never been to Australia, because the flight terrifies me, but I think I would like to go there one day.

d. Make a film. If people like it, you'll be okay. There is no route that I know of.

4. Steve Coogan

a. It's so easy to laugh; it's so easy to hate; it takes guts to be gentle and kind.

b. I don't like big feet, reminds me of gammon.

c. People come up to me in supermarkets and demand humour. And the less amusing I am, the more they piss themselves.

d. Actually the best thing I did was to get thrown out by my wife. She's living with a fitness instructor. He drinks that yellow stuff in tins. He's an idiot.

5. Stephen Daldry

a. If you're a director, remember you're not a writer. And if you're a writer, you're probably not a director. Remember the distinction.

b. What's surprising is how many films are still made with a load of people in silly frocks running around gardens and talking in middle-class accents.

c. I have never been motivated by money in my life. You can't make choices based on what the financial return might be.

d. I am, in fact, Superman. Every morning I wake up and go into a telephone booth and change my costume, and then go to work.

6. Stephen Merchant

a. I don't have any hidden depths; I'm a very superficial person. It's a constant frustration to me.

b. I was trying for years to woo people through humour, but it seems flash cars are much easier.

c. It's a strange myth that atheists have nothing to live for. It's the opposite. We have nothing to die for. We have everything to live for.

d. There's this way pop culture has been rammed down our throats that people think that if they were just in the right place at the right time, they'd be married to Heidi Klum.

7. Steve Davis

a. I don't watch a lot of snooker – I keep an eye on the scores, keep my finger on the pulse without sitting in front of the television all day – and I would never go to a snooker table to practise now.

b. I think it's a great idea to talk during sex, as long as it's about snooker.

c. I am so peed off with the game and I am bored with it. I would rather be planting a few shrubs in the garden.

d. Billiards is very similar to snooker except there are only three balls and nobody watches it.

8. Stephen Hendry

a. I wouldn't come here if I didn't think I could win it. I'd go and play bad golf in Spain instead.

b. I played **** in the first match, **** in the second match, and apart from four frames, **** in this match.

c. To be at the top of my sport you have to have that killer instinct and when I'm at the table I'm an animal.

d. I'm surprised at how close the final was considering how badly I played.

9. Shakin' Stevens

a. My second hit was a flop.

b. Oh yeah, I would have been a coal miner, I would think, if I hadn't had tuberculosis when I was 12.

c. Knickers on the stage were a Tom Jones thing. I did used to get a lot of toys and flowers thrown on the stage though – I don't know why.

d. There was no depth to 'Oh Julie' lyrically but it was a catchy little tune.

10. Steven Gerrard

a. When I die, don't bring me to the hospital. Bring me to Anfield. I was born there and will die there.

b. Don't try to beat the goalkeeper, try to destroy the goalkeeper.

c. I've got absolutely no intention of ever going to play at another club.

d. Aggression is what I do. I go to war. You don't contest football matches in a reasonable state of mind.

TEST No. 274685 • Time limit 5 minutes

TALKING ABOUT THE WEATHER

British people over the age of sixty, and posh Brits of any age, seem genuinely interested in talking about the weather. It's the polite way to prevent a conversation from flat-lining when neither party has anything to say. It is always preferable to an embarrassing silence, or a particular kind of tuneless singing known as 'pom pomming', which older male Brits especially lapse into at the first sign of social discomfort.

1. What is the best way to start a conversation about the weather?

a. Make a bold statement of blindingly obvious fact, e.g. 'It's cold today,' or 'It's foggy.'

b. Express earnest surprise about how the current weather contradicts either the forecast or your own expectations, e.g. 'They said it would be sunny this morning.'

c. State with conviction how the current weather will either change soon or persist for some time, e.g. 'This is set to last all day.'

d. any of the above

2. What is the commonly accepted British attitude towards the rain?

a. Rain is always bad.

b. Rain is nearly always bad (except when the garden needs it).

c. Rain is refreshing and invigorating.

d. 'I don't have a strong opinion about rain.'

3. What phrase should you commonly use to inject a degree of polite optimism into a conversation about precipitation?

a. 'I like rain, actually.'

b. 'It's good for the garden though.'

c. 'At least we don't live in Eritrea.'

d. 'Well, we'll all be dead soon.'

4. **On a hot sunny day, a British person will either tell you 'it's hot' or venture a stronger opinion, such as 'it's too hot'. For the sake of politeness, how should you always respond?**

a. 'Yes, it is.' [puff out cheeks for emphasis and look uncomfortable]

b. 'Can I get you a lukewarm beer?'

c. 'Are you crazy? It's perfect!'

d. 'Would you like to borrow my sun cream, you ham-faced twonk?'

5. **When you can't think of anything else to say, how can you keep the inane conversation flowing?**

a. For once in your life, make a true meaningful connection with this other vulnerable human being with whom you briefly share the planet on your vapid mutual trudge towards the grave.

b. Talk about Brexit.

c. Cheerfully lament that the recent downpour will hamper your best efforts to mow the lawn.

d. Offer a breath mint.

6. **When you think you really have exhausted the topic, how can you squeeze out an extra five minutes of thrilling weather talk?**

a. Make an optimistic or quasi-philosophical weather-related quip such as 'Well, we just have to take what we're given,' or 'Long foretold, long last; short notice, soon passed,' and then stand nodding sagely or chuckling good-naturedly.

b. Casually invite the other person to make a prediction about how the weather will develop in the near future, e.g. 'Do you think the sun will last until the weekend?'

c. Recite from memory the long-range weather forecast for the next five days.

d. any of the above

7. **When you walk into a shop on a cold and windy day, how must you greet the shop assistant?**

a. 'Alwight?'

b. 'Hello, it's cold and windy today.'

c. 'Can I get some orange Rizlas please?'

d. 'Sup?'

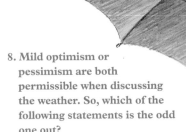

8. **Mild optimism or pessimism are both permissible when discussing the weather. So, which of the following statements is the odd one out?**

a. 'The sun is trying to come out.'

b. 'I think that's it for summer this year.'

c. 'It's so close, we need a storm to clear the air.'

d. 'This humidity is playing havoc with my haemorrhoids.'

9. **Sophisticated weather talk can subtly communicate a Brit's social status. Which of the following are acceptable?**

a. 'Of course, the Range Rover Sport has been an absolute lifeline during the floods.'

b. 'Of course, the sharp frost has been an absolute omnishambles for the Lisianthus and most of the other cultivars.'

c. 'Of course, the humidity has been an absolute clusterf*ck for the jam making.'

d. any of the above

10. **Meteorological small talk is usually expressed with grumpy and apathetic stoicism. Damp weather is the best for British pensioners because it allows them to:**

a. segue into a discussion about arthritis

b. talk about gardening

c. complain about the rising cost of fuel

d. all of the above

TEST No. 274686 • Time limit 2 minutes

THE NHS

Can you help Bernard the D-Day Veteran find his way from the corridor to a hospital bed within eighteen hours before he coughs up a lung?

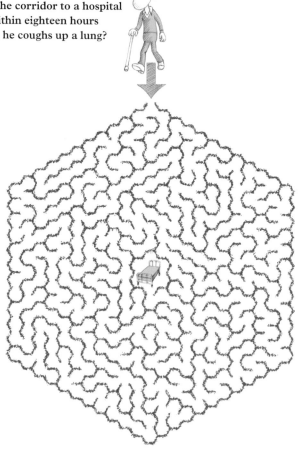

TEST No. 274687 · Time limit 30 seconds

THE WORLD CUP WORD LADDER

It's the same every time the World Cup comes around. Scotland, Wales and Northern Ireland haven't even made the Championships, so the UK's hopes are all pinned on England to rise above their lacklustre form that saw them scrape into the last thirty-two teams that compete for the FIFA World Cup Trophy. Here's a word ladder. See if you can make your way from BLINDLY OPTIMISTIC to SUICIDAL in two short weeks.

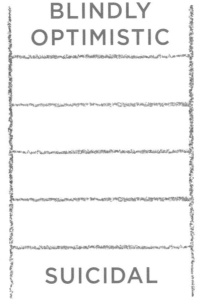

BLINDLY
OPTIMISTIC

SUICIDAL

TEST No. 274688 · Time limit 5 minutes

THE RULES OF BRITISH QUEUING

Brits have a reputation for queuing; it has even been said that they love to queue. If you're a Brit you'll know that's utter nonsense. Nobody loves to queue but, equally, you can't understand why anyone wouldn't when the alternative is chaos. As a post-Brexit Brit, you can feel superior to any nationality that favours an undignified free-for-all over an orderly queue. And it's called a queue, it's NOT a line.

1. For which of the following might you be expected to queue in the UK?

a. public toilet

b. post office

c. tickets for *Last Night of The Proms*

d. all of the above

2. Rank these misdemeanours in order of seriousness (1 worst, 4 least worst).

a. cutting in a queue

b. using a disabled toilet when you're not disabled

c. being fall-down drunk in public

d. throwing a cigarette butt out of a moving car

3. How does queuing work in McDonald's?

a. There's an individual queue at each till, but staff have to repeatedly tell the customers that, as it's not entirely obvious.

b. There is one queue for all tills, leaving a five-foot gap between the front of the queue and the tills.

c. In many branches, the staff usher waiting customers into separate queues during peak hours.

d. all of the above

4. If someone only has a few items at a busy supermarket checkout, when should you let them nip in front of you?

a. quite often

b. only if they are older than me

c. quite often, unless I'm in a hurry, when I will make an

apologetic face or explain that I'm in a hurry

d. only if I'm in a good mood

5. **What's the best thing about queuing?**

a. sharing a polite moan with other queuing strangers

b. thermos flasks, sandwiches and camping chairs

c. decency, democracy and fair play in action

d. all of the above

6. **Under what special circumstances is cutting into a queue or saving a place acceptable behaviour? You may pick more than one answer.**

a. never

b. The person has a disability, which makes queuing very difficult.

c. The person has a disability but it isn't immediately apparent why he or she can't queue up like the rest of us.

d. The queue is for Wimbledon returns or a Black Friday sale, has lasted for several days and the cutter-inner has paid an individual to queue on their behalf.

7. **As if you weren't stupid enough for spending £238 + £5 booking fee for a ticket to Glastonbury Festival, how long would you be willing to queue to get in?**

a. four hours

b. five hours

c. six hours

d. eight hours

8. **Who should get served first at a bar?**

a. the person who has been waiting the longest, observing the principle of 'first come, first served'

b. the guy who waves his money around

c. the prettiest woman or the tallest guy

d. whoever can catch the attention of the barperson most effectively – it's a free-for-all

9. **How many hours does the average Brit spend queuing every year?**

a. 64 hours

b. 32 hours

c. 18 hours

d. 24 hours

10. **According to surveys, after enduring a long queue, what percentage of Brits smile sweetly and tell the cashier it's fine, despite feeling annoyed?**

a. 28%

b. 48%

c. 58%

d. 78%

THE FULL WINDSOR

The Windsor knot is as quintessentially trustworthy and British as bread and butter pudding, so it's ironic that its namesake, King Edward VIII (aka the Duke of Windsor), was a German playboy and Nazi sympathiser who plunged the country into constitutional chaos. In common with most British institutions, to avoid stumbling into an existential crisis, it's best not to scratch too far beneath the surface.

Suffice it to say that the Windsor knot is the epitome of sartorial elegance. It is plump, symmetrical and triangular, and sits teutonically below one's Adam's Apple like a majestic river delta surveying the ocean, except that it's made out of silk-polyester rather than deposited silt. The War was won, *Brideshead Revisited* written and the KitKat invented by Windsor-wearing Englishmen.

It expresses the corpulent self-satisfaction of a nation that once held sway over one-quarter of the world's population. Skinny ties are the preserve of undernourished call-centre drones and Americans called Don (Draper, Trump, Johnson). Silicon Valley has ditched the tie altogether, which makes the Windsor knot even more important, the podgy thumb in the dam to stem the flood of bare-necked transatlantic anarchy.

You have three minutes to execute the perfect Windsor knot like the one shown opposite. Then check to see if you followed the correct procedure. If not, don't be disheartened. The Duke of Windsor cheated by having his ties made with an extra thick lining. Such innate class. You can't buy breeding like that.

ANATOMY OF A KNOT

(A) Top button closed (even Ian Botham and Colin Farrell do this now).

Tie bar attaches between third and fourth button and warns strangers that wearer is tedious company.

Tie bar should be shorter than the width of the tie; longer is gauche, (B) especially when accompanied by matching ballpoint pen.

Tie tip should reach the middle of waistband. Higher = schoolboy; lower = Donald Trump.

Keep waistband below navel.

Diamond tip (square ended ties are only worn by pederasts and/or geography teachers).

Plump centre knot with horizontal top (C).

Crisp point sits on vertical power line.

Thin ties are for Americans and skinny scrotes called Kyle who work in call centres and buy their lunch from Greggs.

(D) Broad centre flare max 6.75 cm (aka the 'kipper event horizon').

TEST No. 274689 • Time limit 5 minutes

WALES

Wales is a proud nation, famed for its rugby, singing and poetry, although in a recent survey by The Principality Building Society, coal was voted its biggest legacy. The majority of people living in Wales identify themselves as being Welsh rather than British, and The United Kingdom Census 2011 recorded that 19 percent of Welsh residents aged three and over can speak Welsh. Wales also boasts some of the most rugged and beautiful landscape in the UK including five Areas of Outstanding Natural Beauty.

1. The last great Welsh invention was the coracle, which is a kind of *what*?

   a. stringed musical instrument

   b. umbrella

   c. soothsayer

   d. boat

2. The Welsh are renowned for their resourceful cookery and will eat practically anything that washes up on their sub-Arctic beaches. Their most famous salvaged cuisine, lava bread is made from what?

   a. number-plates

   b. seaweed

   c. plastic bags

   d. spent heroin needles

3. If they don't have a word for something, the Welsh steal an English word and then:

   a. remove all the vowels and add three 'y's.

   b. add 'dd' to the end.

   c. add 'olio' to the end.

   d. any of the above

4. At rugby matches, instead of chanting 'Come on Wales,' what do Welsh people sing about?

   a. dragons

   b. saucepans

   c. slate

   d. Brains Bitter

5. **Perhaps Wales' most famous contribution to international cuisine is 'Welsh rarebit'. What are its vital ingredients?**

a. toast

b. cheese and egg yolks

c. a fermented anchovy sauce from the West Midlands

d. all of the above

6. **The customary way of thanking someone in Wales is to:**

a. carve a love spoon.

b. buy them a much needed twenty-foot booster aerial for their telly

c. say 'diolch yn fawr'

d. pretend you are coughing up a large fur ball.

7. **How would you describe traditional Welsh pottery?**

a. it is to sophisticated ceramics what the Sons of Glyndwr were to fire safety

b. thick, heavy and ugly

c. looks like it's been made by quadriplegic gorillas

d. all of the above

8. **Until the end of the nineteenth century, what was the traditional Welsh way of celebrating Christmas?**

a. dancing about with a horse's skull on a pole

b. eating slate

c. throwing stones at seagulls

d. exchanging lumps of coal

9. **What is the Welsh word for 'motorway service station'?**

a. Gwasanaethau

b. Gwasananaethau

c. Gwasanananananananananananaethau

d. Gwasananethanau

10. **The Americans have the Smithsonian; the French have the Louvre; Spain has the Prado; the Italians have the Uffizi; the Welsh have:**

a. Tŷ Hyll, The Ugly House on the A5 at Capel Curig

b. Slate Museum, Llanberis

c. Wales Millennium Centre, Cardiff

d. all of the above

11. **True or false: Conway Castle smells of urine.**

a. true

b. false

12. **How on Earth did a deformed onion become a Welsh national symbol?**

   a. It harks back to a time, before the 1990s, when Welsh pagans exclusively worshipped broadleaved vegetables.

   b. In the fourteenth century, the feared Welsh archers wore green and white uniforms at the Battle of Crecy.

   c. According to legend, St. David the Patron Saint of Wales, got the Welsh soldiers to wear leeks in their helmets when fighting the Saxons, so they'd know who was on which side. This apparently led to a great Welsh victory, although why this helped them more than the Saxons, has never been properly explained.

   d. any of the above

13. **The leek is hailed for its medicinal properties, but which of these common ailments does it fail to treat?**

   a. heart disease

   b. blood clots

   c. strokes

   d. being Welsh

14. **What was the collective name for the garrison that withstood a seven-year siege of a castle in North Wales during the Wars of the Roses?**

   a. Treorchy Male Voice Choir

   b. Men of Harlech

   c. Super Furry Animals

   d. Manic Street Preachers

15. **What is the best way to be chivalrous in Wales?**

   a. Put a 'Motorsport' sunstrip on your 1.1 litre Fiesta.

   b. Perform some handbrake turns in a McDonald's car park.

   c. Pretend you like rugby.

   d. Offer to hold the umbrella.

TEST No. 274690 • Time limit 2 minutes

BEING OVERLY POLITE

Being overly polite and apologising frequently come as easily as breathing to a well-brought-up British person who doesn't suffer from asthma. But this doesn't mean they are pushovers, because the flip side of all this surface-deep equanimity is masterful passive-aggression, and that other British secret weapon – irony.

Across

1. 'I'm _____ , but do you have the time?' (finding out what time it is)

2. '_____ , but it's what I believe.' (having an opinion)

3. '_____ , but this doesn't work.' (returning something that's defective)

4. '_____?' (Pardon?)

5. '_____.' (What a British person says when someone gets in their way.)

6. '_____ , but you're wrong.' (polite dissent)

8. '_____ , if I could just say.' (permission to speak)

9. '_____ to bother you.' (a polite interruption)

Down

1. 'I'm _____ , but I've received a better job offer.' (handing in your notice)

2. '_____ , but this mullet isn't cooked.' (sending back your meal)

3. 'I'm _____?' (Did you really just say that?)

4. '_____ , I'm not here. Please leave a message after the tone.' (answer machine)

5. '_____ , could you pass ...' (table manners)

6. '_____ , but I haven't finished.' (standing one's ground)

7. '_____!' (What a British person says when someone steps on their foot.)

TEST No. 274691 • Time limit 3 minutes

PANTOMIME

Few British institutions are harder to stomach than the annual pantomime. Imagine cherry-picking the worst elements from the world of showbiz (or human existence). You still won't come close to the mutant music hall throwback that is panto: the same tired old scripts with a few tabloid contemporary references, Z-list celebrities with fluorescent teeth plastered in orange foundation, talking animals, cross-dressing, garish colours, wigs, sweets and sticky seats, jokes about bottoms, camp innuendo, stage-school children, pratfalls and custard pies, audience participation, and pre-recorded backing music. The biggest slap in the face for the paying punter is that the performers claim they are participating in an 'art form' with a 'long tradition' and 'broad appeal' whose chief merit is that three generations of the same family can suffer together.

Can you find how four groups of four are linked to each other in this grid?

Puss	licking the nuts off a large Neapolitan	Trott	ring
Goose	'Shut up, you annoying twat!'	Dick	Twankey
in my box	Jack	Sara the Cook	'He's behind you!'
'Oh yes she is!'	'Where's the soap?'	'Oh no he isn't!'	wax off

TEST No. 274692 · Time limit 5 minutes

SCOTLAND

Scotland is a fearsome nation, famed for its dark beautiful mountains, purple glens, rich green forests, red faces and ginger pubes, which are worn outside the clothes and called a 'sporran'. The Scottish are famous for two things: not wearing any underpants and inventing stuff, which includes penicillin, the telephone, the television, criminal fingerprinting, swearing, head butting, heart disease, picnic rugs and Dolly the sheep.

1. Which Scottish word for 'small' means 'bladder contents' to everyone else?

a. urine

b. tiny

c. wee

d. yea big

2. What is the Scottish word for eight metres of industrial gauge sheep's wool secured with two buckles and worn without 'kecks'?

a. big girl's dress

b. kilt

c. haggis

d. Tam o' Shanter

3. If you can scribble a few lines of nationalistic doggerel on the back of a cigarette packet, you'll be hailed as a great poet in Scotland. Name the incompetent farmer who wrote pages of gibberish about sheep's intestines and Tam o' Shanters that not even the Scottish can understand.

a. John o' Groats

b. Mel Gibson

c. Robbie Burns

d. Rob Roy

4. What do Scottish people get before boarding public transport?

a. a ticket

b. into a fight

c. drunk

d. tearfully nostalgic about how great the shipyards used to be

5. Name the Scottish city which is the heart attack capital of Europe, where inhabitants exist on a diet of fries, pies and

crisps swilled down with litres of lurid orange fizzy drinks.

a. Perth

b. Edinburgh

c. Aberdeen

d. Glasgow

6. 'Horribly sloppy, contaminated with cancer-causing chemicals and with a texture like raw bacon smeared in Vaseline.' This is an accurate description of which premium Scottish food product?

a. salmon

b. deep fried Mars Bar

c. porridge

d. neeps and tatties

7. What are 'neeps and tatties'?

a. nipples and titties

b. mashed swede and/or yellow turnips and mashed potatoes

c. haggis and boiled potatoes

d. deep fried pizza

8. Name the eighties film set in Scotland in which Christopher Lambert plays a Scot with a French accent and Sean Connery plays an Egyptian with a Scottish accent.

a. *Skyfall*

b. *Tarzan*

c. *Highlander*

d. *Whisky Galore*

9. True or false: everyone in Scotland is either a freemason or an unemployed welder.

a. true

b. false

10. Name the great Scottish hero who was a French side-switching spider-loving mummy's boy who spent half of his life in a cave and the other sucking up to the English aristocracy.

a. Ally McCoist

b. Robert the Bruce

c. Alexander Graham Bell

d. Bruce Forsyth

11. Name the Scottish city that's full of failed actors and yuppies who can't afford to live in London anymore and think Irvine Welsh is worth reading.

a. Edinburgh

b. Stirling

c. Dundee

d. Aberdeen

12. Name three Scottish things that sound like a chain saw with vibrato.

a. bagpipes

b. The Proclaimers

c. Lulu

d. all of the above

13. The Scottish specialise in gibberish expressions like 'Many a mickle makes a muckle'. What does this actually mean?

   a. Many little things add up to a lot.

   b. If you never open your wallet, one day you'll be rich, my son.

   c. Look after the pennies and the pounds will look after themselves.

   d. all of the above

14. What do you get when you stuff a disembowelled sheep back into its own stomach?

   a. indigestion

   b. a haggis

   c. diverticulitis

   d. any of the above

15. Name the Scottish folk hero whose fame was perpetuated and romanticized by Sir Walter Scotch, inventor of turgid historical novels.

   a. Marti Pellow

   b. Rob Roy

   c. Sheena Easton

   d. Midge Ure

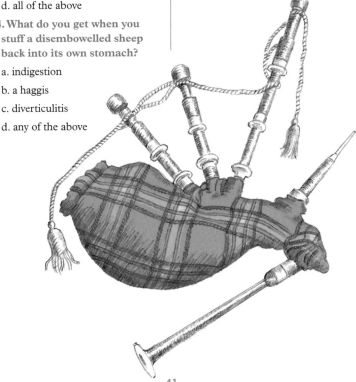

TEST No. 274693 · Time limit 10 minutes

ALL-YOU-CAN-EAT BUFFET

'In Xanadu did Kubla Khan a stately pleasure dome decree …'
If Kubla Khan had the foresight to whack in an all-you-can-eat
world buffet, he could have been coining in more than £10,000
a night. That's if the Xanadusians were even half as gluttonous
as the British, who spend about £4,000 on dining out each year
and love nothing better than stuffing themselves into a near
coma. There are fifty buffet items hidden in the word search
opposite. See if you can find them all (including a hidden
bonus – diabetes), but have a thorough recce before you load
up your plate. Don't fill up on cheap carbs like pizza and chips,
go for protein – seafood and cuts of meat (more expensive =
better value) and the chocolate fountain is the very best return
for your money (it can cost the restaurant £120 a day to run).

basmati	kebab	rogan josh
burger	korma	saag
burrito	madras	samosa
carvery	masala	sausage
chicken	meatball	scotch egg
chicken balls	moussaka	sushi
chips	mutable	scallops
crabsticks	mussels	spaghetti
curry	nacho	spring roll
diabetes	nuggets	tabbouleh
dolmas	pakora	tandoori
drumstick	paella	tempura
fajitas	pasty	teppanyaki
fish and chips	pizza	tikka
frankfurter	prawn	tortilla
gravy	quiche	wings
ice cream	ribs	

```
T G A S O M A S H E L U O B B A T O H J C S
O P P R S A R D A M G G E H C T O C S G J S
R A M E A T B A L L I K A Y N A P P E T E J
T K S T D M U O A B L Z M S A A G K U N U G
I O Q R R N I Q R Z Z C F Z C R S K C X B O
L R Q U U G P M U I O Y R R U C K G V M W Y
L A A F M R O O P R W A N E L B A T U M M N
A A S K S A O U M B W Y G S A M L O D F A R
C M K N T V B S E F A J I T A S N V R I E O
Y R C A I Y U S T P U Y C S L P U V I S R G
R O I R C T R A P R U S H P L N G S B H C A
E K T F K I G K F A Y U I A O Z G C S A E N
V G S T J K E A E W D S C G R A E A I N C J
R A B E W K R G B N O H K H G L T L R D I O
A L A O B A P A H T D I E E N L S L O C Y S
C A R F H A S L I Y I D N T I E T O O H X H
D S C F S M B R V L A W B T R A D P D I S L
G A T W A P R E N Y B H A I P P J S N P G C
Q M M T G U I K K T E S L F S V P R A S N X
G Y I Q B D Q H K S T S L E S S U M T C I I
Y O H C A N P X C A E M S Q U I C H E T W Q
Z E C H I C K E N P S N W T X E G A S U A S
```

TEST No. 274694 • Time limit 30 seconds

WATCHING FOOTBALL DOWN THE PUB

If you're a football moron with a drinking problem and can't afford a season ticket, or Sky Sports, there's a way to yell at your team whilst not financially supporting them – down the pub. Here you can experience all the action and tribal antagonism of a live game, with the added frisson of non-segregated seating (with a rubbish view of the screen) and the chance of being beaten up for cheering the wrong side. You'll lose count of the number of times your pint gets knocked over when a goal is scored or being told by a loudmouth opposition supporter, 'Don't stand next to me wearing that.'

Put your football knowledge to the test in this Spot-the-Chelsea-player challenge. Only one of these guys does not play for Chelsea. Can you guess which one?

TEST No. 274695 • Time limit 5 minutes

BIG BEN

The name Big Ben is often used either in ignorance or as shorthand, to refer either to the tower (which stands at the north end of the Houses of Parliament and was imaginatively named The Clock Tower, then renamed Elizabeth Tower in 2012 to mark the Diamond Jubilee of Elizabeth II) or the clock (which is called the Great Clock of Westminster). Actually it's neither. Big Ben is the nickname of the largest of its five bells, aka the Great Bell. The Victorians didn't waste time thinking up imaginative names. If it was constructed today, public consensus would generate Clocky McClockFace.

The foundation stone for the Elizabeth Tower was laid on 28th September 1843, and the construction was a typical British affair – five years overdue and with spiralling costs (£22,000). It was finally completed in 1859; the clock went into operation on 31st May and Big Ben chimed for the first time on 11th July.

The origin of the name Big Ben is still debated. It could either refer to Sir Benjamin Hall, the Welsh civil engineer and politician who oversaw its installation, or the English heavyweight boxing champion Benjamin Caunt.

FIVE BELLS PUZZLE

A big bell is accompanied by four smaller bells. The big bell chimes once and then chimes again after every single combination of the four smaller bells has been used, including chiming alone and in groups. On which number chime will the big bell chime for the second time?

Big bell   A   B   C   D

TEST No. 274696 • Time limit 5 minutes

THE BEATLES

Is there anything left to say that hasn't already been said about the four scallies from Liverpool who became the most famous people on the planet? John met Paul, they met George, Pete got fired, Ringo got hired, hair grew from mop tops to psychedelic shags, there was lots of screaming and airports and growing of sideburns, Paul died in a car crash, was replaced by a clone, John met Yoko and they stayed in bed and announced it was revolutionary. The group split, John wrote 'Imagine', Paul became a vegan, John got shot, MJ bought their back catalogue – the only sensible purchase he made in his entire life, bless him. Three Beatles grew old, one died and one embarrasses himself every decade by singing off key at international events.

That's it really. Here are some questions.

1. Why was George Harrison initially turned down by John and Paul?

a. He'd only just turned fifteen.

b. He could actually play the guitar, which made them look bad.

c. He was too quiet.

d. They didn't like his rubber soul.

2. Who became their manager in 1961 and secured them a recording contract with EMI?

a. Cilla Black

b. George Martin

c. Gerry Marsden

d. Brian Epstein

3. The group's first single, 'Love Me Do', was released in 1962. What was the 'B' side?

a. 'Please Please Ask Me Why I Saw Her Standing There.'

b. 'You Give Me Norwegian Wood.'

c. 'P.S. I Love You.'

d. 'Do You Want to be Our Drummer?'

4. As Beatlemania intensified, police resorted to using *what* to control the screaming crowd before a concert in Plymouth?

a. Royal Marines

b. high-pressure water hoses

c. tear gas

d. noise-cancelling headphones

5. Released in 1963, their second album, *With the Beatles*, included George's first solo writing credit. What was the name of the song?

a. 'This Money Is I Me Mine'

b. 'Don't Bother Me'

c. 'Roll Over Mr Postman'

d. 'Devil in Her Heart'

6. Visiting the band in their New York hotel suite in August 1964, Bob Dylan introduced the Beatles to *what*?

a. cannabis

b. long hair

c. Maharishi Mahesh Yogi

d. selling out

7. These four remarks by John Lennon genuinely appeared in the same 1966 interview for the London newspaper the *Evening Standard*. Which was the only one to cause extensive protests in the Southern United States?

a. 'Christianity will go. It will vanish and shrink.'

b. 'We're more popular than Jesus.'

c. 'Jesus was all right but his disciples were thick and ordinary.'

d. 'It's them twisting it that ruins it for me.'

8. Which of these tracks appears on the 1967 album *Sgt. Pepper's Lonely Hearts Club Band*?

a. 'With a Little Help from My Stash'

b. 'Lucy in the Sky with Diamonds'

c. 'Here Comes the Fuzz'

d. 'Lovely Reefer'

9. What was the name of their twelfth and final studio album, released a few weeks after the group's break-up?

a. *All Things Must Pass*

b. *Let it Be*

c. *Long and Winding Court Battle*

d. *(We Probably Won't) Get Back*

10. A statue of Eleanor Rigby can be seen on Stanley Street, Liverpool, with the plaque: 'Dedicated to All the Lonely People'. Who designed and made it [for real]?

a. Cilla Black

b. Peter Blake

c. Antony Gormley

d. Tommy Steele

TEST No. 274697 • Time limit 2 minutes

CHEESE ROLLING

Every Spring Bank Holiday, dozens of idiots from all over the world chase a 4kg circular truckle of Double Gloucester cheese down one-in-three Cooper's Hill, near Gloucester. When they reach the bottom, their momentum is halted by a strategically placed row of ambulances with their back doors open. The injured participants keep piling up until each ambulance is full, the doors are kicked shut and they are all driven to hospital to receive electroconvulsive therapy. A handful of the same faces seem to win year after year, so clearly there is some skill involved beyond living in Gloucestershire and having severely impaired frontal lobes.

Which of the six competitors wins the truckle?

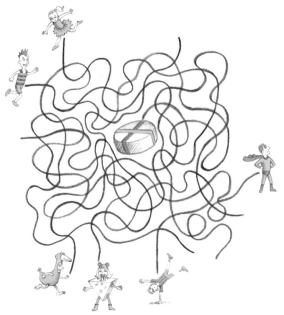

TEST No. 274698 • Time limit 3 minutes

THE GRAND NATIONAL

Can you help hundred-to-one shot Foinavon reach the winning line and plod to victory? There's no hurry because all the other riders have fallen off their horses.

TEST No. 274699 • Time limit 10 minutes

THE GRAND NATIONAL

The most famous National Hunt horse race in the world is held annually at Aintree Racecourse in Liverpool, enjoyed by a nation of supposed animal lovers. Forty horses have to run 4 miles 514 yards and jump 30 fences over two laps, whilst carrying a tiny aggressive Irishman and avoiding injury, otherwise they get shot in the head. First run in 1839, the Equine Hunger Games are watched on television by millions who would cause an outcry if they saw horses being publicly garrotted in Sainsbury's, but glibly plant their entire family in front of this macabre handicap steeplechase in which broken spines, severed tendons and heart failure are par for the course.

There are fifty Grand National items hidden in the word search opposite. See if you can find them all.

Aintree	fences	National Hunt
Auroras Encore	flutter	Neptune Collonges
Ballabriggs	Foinavon	Numbersixvalverde
Becher's Brook	fracture	photo finish
betting	front runner	racehorse
broken ankle	furlong	Red Rum
Canal Turn	green screens	shoot
carnage	Gregalach	shotgun
Caughoo	handicap	Silver Birch
Comply Or Die	heart failure	steeplechase
dangerous	infarction	steward's enquiry
death	injury	The Chair
Don't Push It	jockey	thoroughbred
euthanasia	lethal	Tipperary Tim
false start	Lord Gyllene	whipping
fatalities	Mon Mome	winning post
favourite	murder	

```
C N U M B E R S I X V A L V E R D E G N I P P I H W
Z C B S S P I I W I N N I N G P O S T E I R E M D N
Y J R N Z D N T I P P E R A R Y T I M X L K C Q S M
A C P E C J I N H H I S S G G I R B A L L A B C L T
O O G U U Y A N J T F A V O U R I T E P G X F A K Z
E E S R O H E C A R A S N E E R C S N E E R G U K Q
K O Y E M O M N O M U E S A H C E L P E E T S G F M
D O N T P U S H I T N I D F A T A L I T I E S H E F
C A N A L T U R N E R O C N E S A R O R U A R O N R
E E R U L I A F T R A E H L E T H A L C H Y S O C A
A T H P W B R O K E N A N K L E T H E C H A I R E C
N N R H F O H B X I C S U O R E G N A D S Q F T S T
O U H O G O E E T H O R O U G H B R E D A H R W K U
I H C T C G I G N A E D W S A H A D P O R C O B D R
T L A O F Q Z N A E I P A A V I O G C K M R N N K E
C A L F L G F C A N L S A F L K A Y P A U I T Z T H
R N A I U N T O V V R L A C B E C H E R S B R O O K
A O G N T O O M Z G O A Y N I M T L X N Y R U Y Z D
F I E I T L O P A Z G N C G A D V S O U E E N E M A
N T R S E R H L S F B S V L D H N M D G L V N K U L
I A G H R U S Y A Y O V N F S R T A P T X L E C R U
X N M T V F P O H G S Q L V H T O U H O F I R O D E
E G V W A A G R E E R T N I A Z G L E H Q S T J E U
F S T E W A R D S E N Q U I R Y F A L S E S T A R T
L M U R D E R I U T I J K B E T T I N G D I N R O Y
B Z L Q L N S E G N O L L O C E N U T P E N U P X F
```

TEST No. 274700 • Time limit 5 minutes

LAWNS

Ask an Englishman over the age of thirty what he would like to surround his semi-detached castle and you'll receive the unanimous reply, 'a nice lawn' (women – and even feminists in spite of themselves – have different priorities, like a showcase kitchen). Aside from a sports car or designer chronograph, it's a proper grown-up British male status symbol, demonstrating that one's crippling mortgage extends to more than mere bricks and mortar, and that one is a landowner, a mower, scarifier, aerator and feeder of lawns, a custodian of sovereign British turf, all of which requires leisure time and money. The lawn must be immaculate, otherwise it merely reveals to one's neighbours a chaotic lifestyle, bereft of the wherewithal to maintain a verdant middle-class oasis. How much do you care about your lawn?

1. **How many lawnmowers do you own?**

   a. None – I don't yet have a lawn. (*End quiz here, with sincerest sympathy, and go update your CV.*)

   b. one old, one current, one broken, one robotic, plus two scarifiers

   c. one old, one current

   d. one

2. **Would you say you 'love' your lawn?**

   a. I like the smell of freshly cut grass, if that's what you mean.

   b. I can't wait until I retire so that I can spend more time with it (I'm 28 years old).

   c. It's a love/hate relationship. It will never be perfect.

   d. I'm working at the relationship, but turf is a cruel mistress that gives so little in return.

3. **How much do you hate ants?**

   a. I loathe them with a passion; just as the growing season starts in earnest, those nasty little dirt drones leave piles of soil all over my beautiful lawn, just as it is starting to look nice.

   b. They are a vital and beautiful part of the ecosystem.

   c. Live but let die, is what I say.

   d. The best ant is a dead ant.

4. Do you scarify?

a. Do I scare easily?

b. No mate, life's too short.

c. I use a fine tine rake once every few years.

d. I hum Elgar's Enigma Variations as I, twice yearly, stride up and down pushing my motorised scarifier to fill a builder's sack with thatch and moss for Queen and country.

5. Are there any defunct white goods on your lawn?

a. Nothing is allowed on my lawn, apart from the bird scarer and the 'keep off the lawn' signs.

b. Yes, an old fridge. (*Very British, but just not cricket, old boy – pull your socks up and stop tucking them into your tracksuit trousers.*)

c. No, just a Weber six-burner barbecue and the luxury rattan extended corner sofa combo with matching dining table.

d. No, but there is last year's Christmas tree.

6. Do you suffer from lawn envy?

a. Yes, but that's only because their septic tank is overflowing.

b. Yes, but I don't discuss lawn maintenance with other men; a tip top lawn is just part of my effortless style.

c. The face really is greener on this side on the fence.

d. Not really.

7. How's your edging?

a. My *what*?

b. spade cut, trimmed with nail scissors

c. eroded

d. trimmed weekly with a power edger, bordered with slate chippings

8. How do you approach bare patches?

a. I don't really notice them.

b. I try to fix them, but my lawn always looks like I just hosted the Bath and West Show.

c. with vigorous overseeding

d. I don't have any bare patches.

9. Groundsmen work tirelessly to make grass look amazing but they get paid for it, and a golf course is a lucrative business, so why do you care so much about your lawn?

a. It quietens the voices in my head.

b. It's kind of like trimming your pubes, but the whole neighbourhood can see.

c. I don't bother that much.

d. Simple division of labour; I'm expected to take out the bins and mow the lawn.

10. How does your weed-free pristine lawn make you feel?

a. Tarmac would be less bother, if I'm honest.

b. It makes me feel superior to my neighbour, despite the Bugatti Veyron sitting on his drive.

c. I wear it in front of my house like a tarpaulin of honour. I have tamed nature with my wallet, relentless focus and the contents of my shed.

d. Not much, apart from the occasional loin twinge, which could just be muscle strain.

TEST No. 274701 • Time limit 3 minutes

GOING FOR A NICE WALK

Pensioners Vera and Fred are enjoying a nice walk. Can you help them find their way home in time for Vera's Zumba class?

TEST No. 2746702 • Time limit 1 month

OVERHEARD IN A POSH SUPERMARKET
WORD BINGO

Eavesdropping in the aisles of a luxury supermarket chain can be a great way to gain a sneak preview into other people's lives. Grab yourself a free cup of coffee and tick these winners off your card, or listen out for even better ones.

Darling, do we need parmesan for both houses?	Please don't rummage in the reduced bin darling, someone from the golf club might see you.	Do you have any gluten-free Yorkshire puddings?	I'm telling Daddy you deliberately trod on my foot. These are suede you know.
Ari put that down. Aristotle, I said now.	Mummy, are we doing shopping for the boat as well?	Should we get an emergency stilton?	Oh tosh, I forgot to buy water for the iron.
Noah! You've had enough manchego for one day.	Mu-umm, aren't we out of pomegranate molasses?	Sebastian, stop hitting your sister, or you won't get any brioche!	We'll have to take the rosemary off the focaccia before we feed the ducks, Olivia; they can't digest it!

TEST No. 2746703 • Time limit 1 month

OVERHEARD IN A REGULAR SUPERMARKET
WORD BINGO

Eavesdropping in the aisles of a cheap and cheerful British supermarket retailer can teach you a lot about your fellow humans. Tick these winners off your card, or keep your ears peeled for some game-stopping gems.

Can you lend us your fake ID?	Nah, Kyle, I said the Pot Noodle *multipack*, you div.	Do you do Crunchy Nut Cornflakes without the nuts?	Put that back. You know we only buy three-litre bottles of cider.
No, Lewis! You've had enough monster munch for one day!	Tyler, put down those WKD! Wait until you're 14!	Lend us a fiver or I'll tell her where you got that hickey.	I'm not being funny or nuffing, but how do you eat courgettes?
It's a fruit, Jayden, we don't like it.	This time they better not have ****ing run out of extra slim ****ing filters.	Nah, don't have that. I just found some frozen ones in batter.	Now hurry up and choose, or you'll get a slap.

TEST No. 274704 • Time limit 5 minutes

THE ROYAL FAMILY

The Royal Family are the nation's most famous post-Brexit asset or liability, depending on your point of view. Many believe they are tireless, non-lizard ambassadors who increase tourism and make the country more special than a republic; some consider them to be the ultimate benefit scroungers whose only function is to normalise and institutionalise inequality. You can be British and be firmly placed in either camp, but what sets Brits apart from the rest of the world is their intimate acquaintance with royal foibles and scandals. For instance, everyone in the UK knows which of the Queen's children is a feckless playboy and which one talks to his plants. We just know this stuff, like we know that the Battle of Hastings took place in a field. So this quiz tests your indigenous royal knowledge.

1. **Which of these statements were actually uttered by the Duke of Edinburgh?**

   a. 'I would like to go to Russia very much, although the bastards murdered half my family.'

   b. 'Do you still throw spears at each other?'

   c. 'You are a woman, aren't you?'

   d. 'If you stay here much longer you'll all be slitty-eyed.'

2. **Who was caught on tape in 1992 telling his mistress that he wished he could be reincarnated as her tampon?**

   a. Prince Charles

   b. Prince Andrew

   c. Prince Edward

   d. The Duke of Edinburgh

3. **Which royal had her toe sucked by a Texan businessman?**

   a. Prince Andrew

   b. Sarah Ferguson, Duchess of York

   c. Prince Charles

   d. Diana, Princess of Wales

4. **Which royal hit the headlines aged fourteen by ordering a cherry brandy?**

   a. Prince William

b. Prince Charles

c. Zara Phillips

d. Camilla Parker Pen

5. **Which royal dressed up as a Nazi officer in 2005?**

a. Prince William

b. Princess Michael of Kent

c. Prince Charles

d. Prince Harry

6. **Which royal's father, Baron Gunther von Reibnitz, was an officer in Hitler's SS?**

a. Princess Michael of Kent

b. The Duke of Edinburgh

c. Diana, Princess of Wales

d. Sophie, Countess of Wessex

7. **Who was fined £400 and received five points on her driving licence after being caught speeding 93mph down a dual carriageway in 2001?**

a. Diana, Princess of Wales

b. Zara Phillips

c. Camilla Parker Knoll

d. Princess Anne

8. **Why haven't they disowned Prince Andrew yet?**

a. Why, what's he done?

b. He's adopted.

c. They are all as bad as each other.

d. They are all lizard people from outer space.

9. **What did the tabloids call Prince Andrew in the 1980s?**

a. Andy Pandy

b. Azerbaijan Andy

c. Airmiles Andy

d. Randy Andy

10. **Who was photographed naked playing strip billiards in August 2012?**

a. Camilla Parker Posey

b. Prince Andrew

c. Prince Harry

d. Prince William

TEST No. 274705 • Time limit 10 minutes

SOAP OPERAS

Soap operas are like pantomimes (see page 38), except they are televised, less well acted and there is no audience participation (unless you count sitting on the sofa dribbling). These domestic modern-day morality tales usually involve a highly polarised view of good and evil, a cast of stock characters, family feuds, adultery, baby snatching, house fires, chatting in the pub and fat bald men standing nose-to-nose shouting at each other and invading each other's personal space so completely that in real life someone would end up getting chinned.

There are fifty soap opera items hidden in the word search opposite. See if you can find them all before your frontal lobes shrink to the size of walnuts.

abuse	extramarital affairs	Phil Mitchell
adultery	fighting	Pobol y Cwm
Albert Square	Get outta my pub	Queen Vic
arson	gossip	racial stereotypes
baby snatching	Hollyoaks	ratings
back from the dead	Home and Away	rivalry
Brookside	Ian Beale	Rovers Return
coma	illegitimate	screaming
Coronation Street	jealousy	shouting
Crossroads	Ken Barlow	sobbing
crying	kidnapping	stock characters
Doctors	melodrama	Walford
Dot Cotton	memory loss	Weatherfield
dramatic irony	Mitchell brothers	Who killed Archie
dysfunctional families	murder	Woolpack
EastEnders	Neighbours	yelling
Ena Sharples	omnibus edition	youthful romance

```
C O R O N A T I O N S T R E E T G O S S I P U Z Z P N
W E A T H E R F I E L D P S R O T C O D E T C O M A W
W Y S Y O U T H F U L R O M A N C E S A T D C E E I G
M V R M S T V A R C Y P L L L P A A J E A M K X R I C
D B E E P K B F P O B O L Y C W M S E D M S T C D A I
K C T M E H A N E I G H B O U R S K L E I G Y R R S V
G F C O G L B R H R M A S C D H X A A H T N R Y O A N
E I A R O G Y S O V P R A Q P I X O E T I I L I F R E
X G R Y B I S F B Z B I W T K Y Q Y B M G T A N L A E
T H A L B G N I P P A N D I K O P L N O E A V G A C U
R T H O M E A N D A W A Y M W Z T L A R L R I C W I Q
A I C S G E T O U T T A M Y P U B O I F L Q R G O A D
M N K S V V C G N I M A E R C S F H G K I Z R U M L R
A G C Q M R H S R E H T O R B L L E H C T I M Y N S A
R W O P H Q I S Q O Y M S G C F J G P A H S K I I T M
I J T I J O N V H R D I L Z Z K K X W B F C P O B E A
T G S R G D G U X U L N F E N A S H A R P L E S U R T
A G A B U S E I H C R A D E L L I K O H W S N B S E I
L S E I L I M A F L A N O I T C N U F S Y D C O E O C
A J L W C R T H M U R D E R S H O U T I N G N K D T I
F Y O V X S D A O R S S O R C W O O L P A C K M I Y R
F X T M P J W R W R R T Y S U O L A E J O D F J T P O
A I R B R O O K S I D E O T V A Y R E T L U D A I E N
I W O L R A B N E K L T N O T T O C T O D K U D O S Y
R Y Z S R E D N E T S A E U E I Y G N I B B O S N R F
S N R U T E R S R E V O R R M E R A U Q S T R E B L A
C R N E H X M J M E L O D R A M A L J F G N I L L E Y
```

TEST No. 274706 • Time limit 3 minutes

SOAP OPERAS

Can you help Grant Mitchell return from Portugal to Albert Square to have a scrap with his brother without getting nose-to-nose with anyone else or setting fire to a pub?

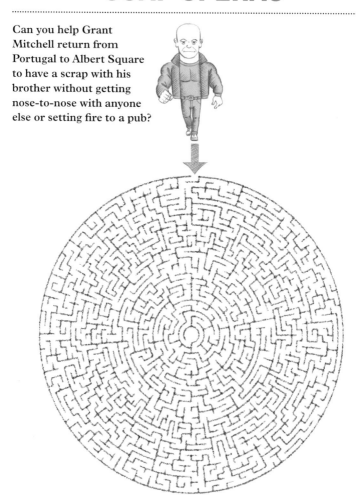

TEST No. 274707 • Time limit 5 minutes

ENGLAND

The English are a people bereft of an empire, but not of the ideals that led to it. When they go abroad, they eat English food, complain about the heat and criticise the television for being in a foreign language. At least fifteen million of them are a bunch of whining Brexiteer nimbies who hate anything that jolts them out of their repetitive, reactionary, safe little sterling-in-my-pocket-stuff-the-euro-I'm-all-right-Jack island mentality.

1. **What is the most popular sexual position for an English male?**

   a. missionary

   b. auto-erotic asphyxiation

   c. sleeping drunk on the couch

   d. drinking warm beer

2. **Name three of the most boring sports in the world that the English invented and now play badly.**

   a. rugby

   b. football

   c. cricket

   d. golf

3. **Speak to any English male and he will tell you how he:**

   a. had trials for Arsenal as a kid, but got a knee injury that ended his career

   b. passed selection for the Parachute Regiment, but got a knee injury that ended his career

   c. used to play golf off scratch, but got a knee injury that ended his career

   d. experienced all of the above.

4. **For a young Englishman, being 'one of the lads' is more important than:**

   a. drinking fewer than nine pints

   b. keeping your arse inside your trousers for ten minutes at a time

   c. showing a modicum of respect for other people's sexual orientation or cultural differences

   d. all of the above.

5. **Every April, the English worship their patron Saint George as the embodiment of all that is English, when in fact he:**

   a. was born in Turkey

   b. wasn't a knight

   c. didn't kill a dragon (because they don't exist)

   d. never visited England.

6. **The English don't have a national dress – they have four. Can you name them?**

7. **Why do the English speak the worst English anywhere in the world?**

   a. The rich ones consider a speech impediment to be a sign of good breeding.

   b. The Ben Sherman/Hackett/ Rockport-wearing plebs punctuate every sentence with 'innit' and 'you're avvin a laugh, intcha?'.

   c. The general masses are fiercely proud of their regional identity, causing them to elongate their vowels, invent their own words for everything and name all their towns after cakes.

   d. all of the above

8. **Why don't English people mind being served warm beer?**

   a. They spend most of the time tipping it over their heads.

   b. They prefer to drink the contents of each other's bladder.

   c. They've already preloaded twenty units at home before they even reach the pub.

   d. all of the above

9. **The BNP and Britain First apparently haven't a clue that they are a mixture of German (Saxons), Scandinavians (Vikings) and French (Normans). Even the 'English' motto is French. What is it?**

   a. the official language spoken by French people

   b. 'L'amour et l'amitié'

   c. 'Dieu et mon Droit'

   d. 'Je ne regrette rien'

10. **The English love their puddings. Which of these delicious English puddings is the odd one out?**

    a. summer pudding

    b. treacle pudding

    c. black pudding

    d. spotted dick

11. **Whenever it's sunny, millions of English families demonstrate their collective idiocy by:**

    a. believing the tabloid weather forecast that the heat wave will last for three weeks

b. dragging a caravan down the M5 for a cream tea in Devon

c. sitting on a beach until their skin starts sloughing off

d. talking endlessly about how hot it is.

12. The English national flower is a typically hazy inter-tribal compromise arrived at in the fifteenth century by Henry VII to stop a civil war between the Lancastrians (who loved white roses) and the Yorkists (who loved red ones). It is:

a. an aspidistra

b. a red rose with a white centre

c. a white rose with a red centre

d. a pink rose.

13. Black pudding, tripe and onions, ox-cheek and kidney pie, faggots: an Englishman's love of eating offal is second only to:

a. The Scottish

b. The French

c. Bolivians

d. Poles

14. Upper-middle-class English people love these four things more than anything. Rank them in order of preference, with 1 being the most important.

a. Brabantia bin

b. farmers' markets

c. Ocado

d. Tuscany

15. Working-class English people love these four things more than anything. Rank them in order of preference, with 1 being the most important.

a. being working class

b. telling people they're working class

c. soap operas

d. self-catering European package holidays

TEST No. 274708 • Time limit 10 minutes

PIGEON FANCYING

Keeping, breeding and racing vermin is said to be both a science and an art. The sport of pigeon racing appeals to people from all walks of life, but those who practise this ancient hobby are commonly known as Yorkshiremen, they number about 60,000 and most of them are called Norman. It can be a lucrative sport, with racing champions changing hands for tens of thousands of pounds, but it demands a strict regime of feeding and exercise, and that's just the owners. You also need to own a shovel and lots of baskets.

There are fifty pigeon fancying items hidden in the word search opposite. See if you can find them all before it's time to muck out the loft again.

airborne	excreta	respiratory disorders
avian tuberculosis	feathers	salmonella
bacterial gastroenteritis	fleas	shoe covering
banding	hepatitis	squeaker
baskets	histoplasmosis	straggler
bird flu	homing	ticks
bloodline	listeriosis	toxoplasmosis
breeder	loft	training toss
campylobacteriosis	mask	transmittable disease
candidiasis	moulting	treading the hen
clutch	navigation	trichomoniasis
cryptococcosis	Newcastle disease	typhoid
dovecote	pathogens	widowhood
droppings	peregrine falcon	wooden lathe
dysentery	pigeon	yearling
E.coli	protective gloves	Yorkshire
eggs	psittacosis	

```
T R I C H O M O N I A S I S S O T G N I N I A R T C W
Q G S S E S A E S I D E L B A T T I M S N A R T Y V I
A O I I T Z S I S O C C O C O T P Y R C D T K E P U D
C Z S S J J X H R E H T A L N E D O O W Y A S Y H L O
I J O O N R K U G B B L O O D L I N E V S P H N O L W
C D C L D G V L I D O X F L D S F K S K E R Z S I O H
L F A U O X N O A A R R H E I F H I F G N P L Q D F O
U S T C V N M I C T T O N O P S S W N T T V P U V T O
T O T R E O C Z L E X K P E M O T I D Z E O Y E S Q D
C W I E C E O S G R I B Q P I I T E Y K R G O A Z E R
H C S B O G B X X C A H E R I L N V R K Y T I K K Y D
I A P U T I C K S X G E E G U N C G O I R E D E E R B
L N Y T E P L P N E Z T Y O J H G P L G O W S R L Y S
U D H N U I Y T T V C A M W I S E S U U F S F O I F A
G I B A C T E R I A L G A S T R O E N T E R I T I S L
N D L I I X P X B P X R T Y E R I H S K R O Y S N U M
I I E V K H G O A Z A O H G S H O E C O V E R I N G O
D A Q A U L L T V V P T R E A D I N G T H E H E N D N
N S K E U Y H I H L R I S T R A G G L E R R A S H O E
A I T C P O U A A B N O K B N J H E P A T I T I S V L
B S L M G L M S D E E S A E S I D E L T S A C W E N L
H P A E F K M N F N S S I L O C E V A K C K B M K S A
H C N D L O C A T Z K R T O X O P L A S M O S I S H A
T S R S S J L V J E Q L M E N A V I G A T I O N V H Y
J I V I G C Z V T X F E A T H E R S H M S N J X D N E
B K S E O G P S R E D R O S I D Y R O T A R I P S E R
H Q H N N M E F L E A S E V O L G E V I T C E T O R P
```

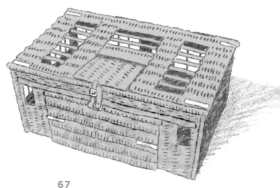

TEST No. 274709 • Time limit 10 minutes

WIMBLEDON

SW19, where the play is hot, the strawberries are cold and expensive, and the queues for returns disappear over the horizon. Every year, The Wimbledon Championships are held over a fortnight at The All England Lawn Tennis and Croquet Club, and is the only Grand Slam tennis event in which British also-rans, John Lloyd and Tim Henman, can get a gig as telly pundits.

Across

2. Grumpy Wolverhampton Wanderers supporter who commentates on Wimbledon for the BBC. (4, 5)

4. Thing that Tim Henman conspicuously failed to reach. (7, 5)

8. Former British Number One who used to eat three eggs, three pieces of toast, all with Bovril on every morning before playing at Wimbledon. (3, 6)

9. Presenter: institute legal procedures against a dog? (cryptic) (3, 6)

10. Former British Number One, whose eyes are too close together. (3, 6)

11. Spanish professional tennis player who adjusts himself between every point. (6, 5)

12. Colour of Boris Becker's eyelashes. (6)

13. Former British Number One and BBC pundit who talks with such self-assurance about the singles final, you'd be mistaken for thinking he actually reached one. (3, 6)

Down

1. Singer who 'entertained' the crowd when rain stopped play. (5, 7)

3. Former British Number One who owns more than 1,000 bottles of wine. (3, 6)

5. The most irritating thing about Maria Sharapova. (5)

6. Former British Number One who has admitted to cracking his knuckles too much. (3, 6)

7. In 1901, his great-grandmother, Ellen Stanwell-Brown became the first woman to serve overarm at Wimbledon. (3, 6)

11. Where the celebrities and posh people sit on Centre Court. (5, 3)

13. hem tinman? (anagram) (3, 6)

WIMBLEDON

Can you work out which four groups of four
are linked to each other in this grid?

Rafael Nadal	Serena Williams	20°C	Chairs
Maria Sharapova	1974	Victoria Azarenka	Gustavo Kuerten
Slazenger	Novak Djokovic	Yellow	1986
David Ferrer	Changing Ends	90 Second Commercial Breaks	Elena Baltacha

TEST No. 274711 • Time limit 5 minutes

NORTHERN IRELAND

Northern Ireland is a welcoming nation, famed for its dark stout, dark hedges, golden whiskey, its many Green Flag winning sites and its proud shipbuilding heritage; with its capital as the place where the unsinkable RMS *Titanic* was built. It is said that Snow Patrol draw their inspiration for their repetitive dirge songs from the sound of riveting on the sandbanks. The Northern Irish are famous for many things, including Eamonn Holmes, lighting bonfires, looking for the craic, drinking Guinness, marching, mural painting and being extras in *Game of Thrones*®. The seat of the Northern Ireland Assembly is called Stormont and politicians take turns sitting down in what's called a 'seat sharing agreement'.

1. What is the name of the famous Irish whiskey brewed in County Antrim?

a. Jameson

b. Bushmills

c. Peaky Blinder

d. Tullamore Dew

2. Ireland is famous for producing alcoholic sportsmen. Which of these two bad boys are from Northern Ireland?

a. George Best

b. Roy Keane

c. Pat Eddery

d. Alex Higgins

3. St Patrick famously drove all the snakes out of Ireland. What vehicle did he use?

a. Range Rover Mk1

b. Morris Marina

c. Vauxhall Viva

d. Austin Allegro

4. Why is the American fantasy drama television series *Game of Thrones*® filmed in Belfast and across Northern Ireland?

a. It's cold, wet and windy.

b. lots of craggy faced alcoholic actors on the doorstep

c. stunning scenery, but you're never too far from a pub

d. all of the above

5. **One of the country's main tourist attractions is an igneous rock formation. What is its name?**

   a. Cribbs Causeway

   b. The Giant Basalt Cash Cow

   c. Giant's Causeway

   d. Finn MacCool's Crazy Patio

6. **Which Northern Irish singer-songwriter is known as 'Your Man with a Van'?**

   a. Neil Hannon

   b. Van Morrison

   c. Gary Lightbody

   d. Duke Special

7. **Which legendary Northern Irish punk pop group was fronted by Feargal Sharkey?**

   a. The Underpants

   b. The Men They Couldn't Stand

   c. Dried Plums with Blue Balls

   d. The Eejits

8. **Which ballix ship was built in Belfast's Harland & Wolff shipyard?**

   a. Amoco Cadiz

   b. Mary Celeste

   c. RMS Titanic

   d. Exxon Valdez

9. **What underwhelming National Trust tourist attraction near Ballintoy in County Antrim has** a staggering 250,000 visitors a year?

   a. Carrick-a-Rede Rope Bridge

   b. Ballycastle Tyre Swing

   c. Coleraine Crawl Through Balloon Tunnel

   d. Dunseverick Tree House

10. **Northern Ireland's most famous export is Stephen Rea. Which movie earned him the Academy Award for Best Actor?**

    a. *The Crying Game*

    b. *Schindler's List*

    c. *How the Other Half Lives*

    d. *It's Not Me, It's You*

11. **The Northern Ireland Championships for which sport take place annually at Peatlands Park in County Armagh?**

    a. bog snorkelling

    b. mud curling

    c. peat digging

    d. fadge eating

12. **Who or what is said to haunt Ballygally Castle?**

    a. The ghost of Lady Isobel Shaw

    b. George Bernard Shaw

    c. One of Eamonn Holmes's silent-but-deadlys

    d. Jedward

13. **What is the craic and why is everybody in Ireland looking for it?**

    a. originally from the Old Northern English and Scots dialect

    b. Jamie Dornan

    c. having a laugh

    d. increasingly commoditised Irish theme pubs

14. **What is The Giant's Ring at Ballynahatty, just south of Belfast?**

    a. geothermal hot spot

    b. Neolithic henge site

    c. prehistoric sinkhole

    d. your nan's gravy

15. **What are The Dark Hedges?**

    a. the Belfast sense of humour

    b. beautiful old gnarly beech trees along Bregagh Road

    c. the Kingsroad in *Game of Thrones*®

    d. chocolate poke (ice cream)

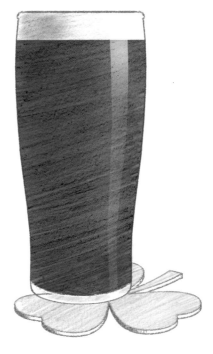

TEST No. 274712 • Time limit 10 minutes

FOR THE LOVE OF RADIO 4

Radio Four, the jewel in the crown of BBC programming,
is a speech-based news and current affairs network aimed
squarely at Middle England. Originally launched in 1967, as
the BBC Home Counties Service, such is the status of this
national institution that it is rumoured that one of the key
tests of imminent civil war is if John Humphrys can no longer
afford to wipe his backside with fifty-pound notes.

Across

2. Arts programme that has benefited greatly from the death of Ned Sherrin. (5, 3)

6. Tedious serial drama about sighing farmers. (3, 7)

7. Sinusely-challenged, soporific host of *In Our Time*. (6, 5)

8. Lame topical comedy show broadcast on Friday evenings. (3, 4, 4)

9. Veteran host of *From Our Own Correspondent*, who sounds like an irate deputy head teacher. (4, 4)

11. Clare Balding yomps around the countryside, talking incessantly. (9)

13. Programme in which posh WI women ask an expert panel questions intended to show off the size of their gardens. (9, 8, 4)

14. The actual length of *Woman's Hour* in minutes. (5, 4)

Down

1. Consumer advice programme that's always about stupid pensioners who've been scammed. (3, 3, 5)

3. Current affairs programme whose presenters are no longer allowed to interrupt filibustering politicians for fear of receiving complaint letters from gammon-faced listeners. (5, 9)

4. Horoscopes for boats? (8, 8)

5. Host of *Any Questions*; the Dimbleby brother who can't get on the telly. (8)

8. Comedy series in which Jeremy Hardy is contractually obliged to spend the first ten minutes upstaging all the other guests. (3, 3, 4)

10. Weekly programme in which the Reverend Richard Coles always manages to mention that he used to be in The Communards. (8, 4)

12. Milton _____. Wearer of loud shirts and cringe-worthy purveyor of deadpan whimsy. (5)

TEST No. 274713 • Time limit 5 minutes

HOW MUCH DO YOU HATE THE FRENCH?

The French are a proud nation, although every time there's a world war, you'd never know it. During the last great conflagration, despite having the Maginot Line and one of the most advanced and mechanised armies in the world, they handed over their country to the Nazis after a mere six weeks of conflict. Then Jean-Paul Sartre and his acolytes spread existential angst and moral relativism around Europe, inspired by the fact that the war they hadn't just fought was pretty unpleasant, declaring that God was dead and had never existed in the first place, as if everyone wasn't miserable enough already. So how much do you hate the French? Answer *true* or *false* to the following thirty statements. The more questions with which you agree, the more you … well you get the picture.

1. They serve salad at the end of the meal, and cheese after you've just eaten the salad you didn't want, and bitter ice cream between every course. They eat live horses, gastropods and amphibians, and drink watered-down wine all day.

2. They wear black turtle-neck sweaters and bright anoraks during the summer.

3. Their language is full of impenetrable grammar and hyperbolic pouting. For example, 'What a shame' in French translates to 'Quelle catastrophe!' They don't even have their own words for most things, (not surprising for a nation that has elevated gesticulating to an art form). For example, the French for chewing gum is 'le chewing gum'.

4. Drugs are so prevalent in their national sport that it is not uncommon for cyclists' heads to explode during the Alpine stages of the Tour de France.

5. In the eleventh century, William the Bastard invaded England just to earn himself a more flattering

nickname. Then he got his half-brother, the bishop of Bayeux, to commission 230 feet of cross-stitch to boost his public image, and set about erecting Norman castles everywhere. A thousand years later, British tax-payers are still picking up the bill for these crumbling Grade One listed ruins.

6. Gauloise cigarettes – the only things that reek worse than the vinegar-stroke-scented rind of Camembert cheese.

7. Everyone owns a poodle but is too cool to scrape their mess off the pavement.

8. They think Jerry Lewis is a comic genius.

9. They brain-farted postmodernism: art lacking any form or content and lots of insideout buildings.

10. They love the accordion, because fleeing from an advancing army is hard when you're carrying a grand piano.

11. They invented sadism, the guillotine, student riots and the metric system.

12. Someone stole all the toilet bowls from their public conveniences.

13. Parisian waiters take twenty minutes just to bring a glass of water.

14. Founded by the French poet and critic André Breton, the Surrealist movement was the inspiration for some of the worst album covers of the seventies. It has encouraged subsequent generations of teenagers worldwide to believe that whatever rubbish they write or draw, directly from their unconscious mind, represents a pure and worthy act of free expression.

15. Even though their national drink – pastis – tastes like mouthwash, nobody over the age of fifty has more than six teeth left.

16. The official symbol of France is a cock.

17. The only war they have ever won was the French Revolution, which was against themselves. They are the only country to ever lose two wars to the Italians.

18. Not content to eat mushrooms that grow above the ground, like everyone else, the French have turned truffles into a gastronomic Holy Grail. They have named them 'Black diamonds' even though they more closely resemble a dog's nose. You can't even find them without a pig.

19. They gave the Americans the Statue of Liberty and kept the Eiffel Tower for themselves (which in any case is a rip off of the one in Blackpool).

20. They didn't have a word for 'humour' (*l'humour*) until 1932, because they prefer pouting and shrugging to laughter.

21. You never know how many times you're supposed to kiss them.

22. The French inflicted bikinis on the world but stubbornly refuse to wear them.

23. The French love regional bureaucracy (one word they actually did invent). The whole nation is devolved into regions, departments, districts, municipalities, villages, cafes, booths, and floor tiles.

24. Ever since the Lumière brothers invented the first movie camera, the French have churned out ponderous self-conscious films featuring men with white socks, and heavy-lidded, flat-chested women brooding on beds chain smoking, endlessly talking and occasionally taking off their clothes.

25. Their national anthem was stolen from that bit at the beginning of 'All You Need Is Love'.

26. Their most important national holiday commemorates the sacking of an almost empty prison, and the murder of six unarmed soldiers and a French governor who had already surrendered.

27. They force feed geese and then suck their livers through a straw.

28. They treat their intellectuals like celebrities, rather than the other way round (like the rest of Europe).

29. Just because they can't add up (they don't have a word for 'eighty' but instead say 'four-twenties' and they can't decide whether there are three or four musketeers), Blaise Pascal invented the first digital calculator, buggering up humankind's ability to do mental arithmetic forever.

30. They are sex mad. Even their bread is phallic.

TEST No. 274714 • Time limit 1 barbecue

HAVING A BARBECUE IN THE RAIN
WORD BINGO

By the time a Brit hangs up his or her barbecue tongs for the last time and heads for that great patio decking in the sky, he or she will, on balance, have experienced significantly more rainy barbecues than sunny ones. Soggy burgers and emergency retreats to the kitchen are simply a fact of life in old Blighty, where you are just as likely to get trench foot in July as in February.

The next time you have a barbecue on your newly sovereign patio, tick these winners off your card.

Are they supposed to be that pink?	Is it ok to barbecue in the garage?	I forgot to buy ketchup.	Just scrape off the black bits.
It won't light.	Sorry, I forgot to mention I'm veggie.	I'd better finish the chicken off in the microwave.	There should have been one each.
Did you actually see the dog lick it?	Put up the parasol, it's starting to rain.	Relax, a little campylobacter never hurt anyone!	Do these sausages look done to you?

TEST No. 274715 • Time limit 5 minutes

STONEHENGE

When some Late Neolithic tribes built this circular arrangement of standing stones on Salisbury Plain in Wiltshire, they couldn't possibly have imagined that 5,000 years later it would still be underwhelming tourists from all over the world and causing unnecessary tailbacks both ways on the A303.

Its original purpose remains shrouded in mystery but there are several possibilities which include: a burial site, healing spa, winter solstice rave venue, observatory to predict eclipses of the Sun and Moon, a colossal hippy magnet, or an Arts Council-funded outdoor art installation. The sophisticated engineering required to transport the famous bluestones from the Welsh Preseli Hills 150 miles away has caused many to speculate that the technology was provided by extraterrestrials, missing the obvious fact that the journey from South Wales to Wiltshire is mostly downhill.

How much do you know about Stonehenge?

1. **Work began around 5,000 years ago, but why did it take over 1,000 years to complete?**

   a. The builders kept disappearing to do other jobs.

   b. Like any publicly funded project, costs spiralled out of control.

   c. They kept having to wait for approval from the local tribal authority building control.

   d. It was badly damaged during the Old Testament flood.

2. **Archaeologists believe the finishing touches were made around 1,500 BC. What were they?**

   a. asbestos cladding

   b. fluoro-resin stone protection

   c. anti-druid spikes

   d. log roll borders

3. **Local businessman Cecil Chubb won Stonehenge at an auction in 1915 (and later gifted it to the nation). How much did he pay for it?**

a. ten shillings

b. He swapped it for his collection of naughty cigarette cards.

c. £6,600

d. one thousand Guineas

4. The average Stonehenge sarsen weighs 25 imperial tons, which is equivalent to how many grains of rice?

a. 205,650,000,000

b. 2,450,000,000

c. 1,650,000,000

d. a mere 850,000,000

5. 50,000 school children visit Stonehenge for free each year, which is equivalent to how many grains of rice?

a. 66,926,043,870

b. 66,926,043,871

c. 66,926,043,872

d. 66,926,043,873

6. 25,335 *what* are eaten at the Stonehenge Visitor Centre each year?

a. packets of crisps

b. rock cakes

c. scones

d. grains of rice

7. How many pagans and hippies turn up at Stonehenge each year to celebrate the summer solstice?

a. between 25,000 – 35,000

b. fewer than 10,000

c. too many

d. between 12,000 – 15,000

8. In 1802, an archaeologist left *what* under the Slaughter Stone for future archaeologists to enjoy?

a. a manuscript copy of Ludwig van Beethoven's 'Moonlight Sonata', which was published in the same year

b. a bottle of port, which was undrinkable when dug up 121 years later

c. a sign saying 'I woz here'

d. a copy of William Wordsworth's poem 'Westminster Bridge'

9. How many people propose to their loved one at Stonehenge each year?

a. fewer than you'd think

b. more than you'd think

c. fewer than thirty

d. about eight thousand

10. There is a controversial £1.4bn plan to build *what* under Stonehenge?

a. glass viewing gallery

b. road tunnel

c. hippy rehab centre

d. crystal healing spa

TEST No. 274716 • Time limit 10 minutes

CASUAL AND INSTITUTIONAL PREJUDICE

Following the Brexit Referendum, the Windrush scandal and numerous instances of high profile British establishment figures making offensive remarks, sadly 'casual and institutional prejudice' must be now included in a list of typically British things.

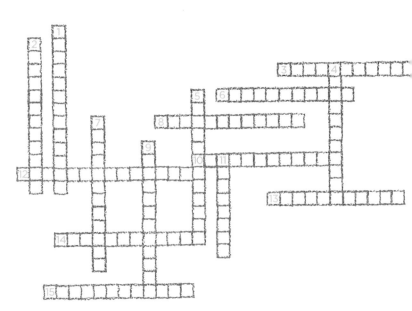

Across

3. MP for Cannock Chase who helped organise a Nazi-themed stag party. (5, 6)

6. British MEP who blamed immigrants for making him late to a meeting. (5, 6)

8. Former London Mayor who referred to black people as 'piccaninnies'. (5, 7)

10. Leicestershire Tory councillor who said that Romanians would 'stick a knife in you as soon as look at you'. (6, 6)

12. Pendle councillor who was sacked for posting a joke on Facebook comparing an Asian man to a dog, and then reinstated so that her party could take control of the council. (8, 7)

13. Maidenhead councillor who suggested that Travellers should be executed. (4, 7)

14. Former London Mayor who pontificated on 'part-Kenyan' Barack Obama's 'ancestral dislike' of Britain. (5, 7)

15. Former London Mayor who, when editor of *The Spectator*, allowed a column to run stating: 'Orientals … have larger brains and higher IQ scores. Blacks are at the other pole.' (5, 7)

Down

1. Tory MP who was condemned for suggesting British women of colour shouldn't criticise the royal wedding and should: 'appreciate the country you benefit from'. (6, 7)

2. Former London Mayor who helped launch the notorious 'Keep Havering Safe' campaign, which warned that the influence of London Mayor, Sadiq Khan, could lead to the borough ending up 'resembling Hackney, Newham, Camden and Barking' rather than 'traditional' parts of Essex. (5, 7)

4. British MEP who said he'd be concerned if his neighbours were Romanian. (5, 6)

5. The government minister who said black people had 'bad moral attitudes'. (6, 6)

7. Orpington councillor who complained that none of the prospective parliamentary candidates 'has a normal English name'. (5, 7)

9. Former London Mayor who referred to black people as having 'watermelon smiles'. (5, 7)

11. Dover councillor who called Middle Eastern people 'sons of camel drivers'. (3, 5)

TEST No. 274717 • Time limit 10 minutes

WATCHING CRICKET

Cricket is the perfect sport for the kind of sports lover who simultaneously has nothing better to do, but does in fact have several things that need urgent attention, like filling in a tax return, doing the Telegraph crossword or sleeping. The geologically slow action on the field means that a person can be said to be 'watching' cricket whilst being in a coma. Even the commentators recognise that it is objectively boring, because they spend most of their time speculating about if, and when, the players will break for lunch. In no other sport do players have sufficient time to tamper with the ball. There are fifty cricket items hidden in the word search below. See if you can find them all before rain stops play.

Ashes	duck	nightwatchman
bad light	Duckworth-Lewis	one day international
bails	fielder	opener
batsman	full toss	over
beamer	glove	rain
bodyline	googly	snickometer
boring	helmet	sticky
boundary	howzat	stumps
bowled	infield	tampering
box	innings	tedious
caught	inswinger	umpire
caught behind	interminable	unexciting
century	jaffa	wearisome
crease	lacklustre	wicket
daisy cutter	lunch	yawn
dibbly dobbly	maiden	yorker
dismissal	monotonous	

```
U N E X C I T I N G S N I C K O M E T E R B Q
G L O V E W E A R I S O M E T H G I L D A B S
F U L L T O S S R L L S G N I N N I O X L U I
U X E J E F C L A S S I M S I D Y P Y O M V W
Y O B R R A C A Z J H I K Q X G X R I P K Q E
L B O E T J S A K C D J D Y H E A T I E I E L
B Y W T S W S H U K E G G H L D C R B N N L H
B A L T U H I O E G X Z E K N G E U N E S B T
O W E U L M N C X S H L T U G K O W K R W A R
D N D C K V I I K F M T O H B T P O K O I N O
Y I R Y C R E M A E B B B B A I L S G T N I W
L N L S A W G N T R T A A E G V T Y S H G M K
B F A I L D B N X I X T H T H Z X D P G E R C
B I C A E P O A C B S H M X A I U P M U R E U
I E G D S J D D X M T O Y A T M N R U A B T D
D L N L A A Y T A E F W X R I O P D T C Q N N
T D I O E F L N R Y C Z O E U D F E S A M I T
E R R I R F I L N I X A B E D T E I R P X K Z
D E O G C A N U V I S T I C K Y N N E I S W R
I K B A L E E N Q E B E F W A W J E H L N A E
O R K C U D D C S U O N O T O N O M C N D G V
U O F P N I G H T W A T C H M A N Y T H F E O
S Y U L A N O I T A N R E T N I Y A D E N O R
```

TEST No. 274718 • Time limit 3 minutes

GOING FOR A CURRY

Gary has drunk ten pints of lager. Can you help him find his way from the pub to the curry house before he passes out in the street?

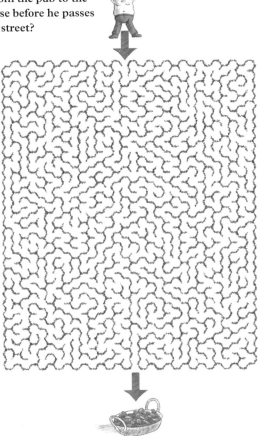

TEST No. 274719 • Time limit 5 minutes

CHEERING THE UNDERDOG

Many people have attempted to explain the nation's curious affinity for the underdog. It seems crazy to root for the team or individual who is most likely to lose, and send us plunging into despair. Maybe we're a nation of gamblers who prefer to place all our chips on the long shot, in return for a bigger pot of happiness if the underdog beats the odds and wins. Or maybe the hurt is less when we're forced to witness the inevitable defeat. Can you identify these twelve underdogs?

Slowest swimming heat winner in Olympic history	Scottish singer, now looks like Harry Styles	Balletic coalminer's son	Maurice Micklewhite's 1964 star debut
Bad bobsleigh team	Middle-earther with a hot ring	Golden ticket winner	Croatian Wimbledon wild card
Rubbish ski jumper	Greedy orphan	Philadelphia boxer	King power 2016

TEST No. 274720 • Time limit 1 minute

CREAM TEAS

A cream tea is a traditional light afternoon meal consisting of a warm scone, clotted cream and strawberry jam. The order in which the jam and cream are applied to the scone has been the main topic of dispute between the people of Devon and Cornwall ever since the two counties mutually agreed that the Earth is flat, that Nigel Farage is their saviour and anyone who shaves their unibrow should be publicly flogged for trying to better themselves.

One of these is a Devonshire cream tea, one is known as a Cornish cream tea and the other one fell on the floor. Do you know which is which?

TEST No. 274721 • Time limit 1 journey

THE LONDON UNDERGROUND

Why is it so hard to get out of quicksand? Is it a solid or a liquid, or both? The overcrowding on the capital's subterranean hellhole, presciently called The Tube, proves that it's certainly possible for human beings to inhabit two states of matter at the same time – a mixture of the corporeal and pure running sweat. Every time the doors open and another impossible slab of humanity oozes into the carriage, the psychic airwaves are filled with silent screams and yet still everyone avoids eye contact, as if to acknowledge the presence of another individual amongst the amorphous swathe of flesh would throw into stark relief the absurdity of this communal excrucitation.

The next time you have the pleasure of becoming a non-Newtonian fluid, play a round of Underground Bingo and spot these twelve individuals to help you forget that you're all merely human oobleck.

Manspreader	Alcoholic	Smells of urine	Posh-quilted-jacket twat
Talking too loudly	Tourist with huge suitcase/backpack	Forces open doors	Sleeping
Feet on seats	Pole hogger	Body odour	Refuses to move down the aisle

TEST No. 274722 · Time limit 10 minutes

NAMING CAKES AFTER NORTHERN TOWNS

This sceptred isle is a foodie paradise, made even more enticing by the plethora of famous comestibles named after their place of origin. As comedian Stewart Lee once remarked, 'And what I say to the people in the North of England is not every town has to have a cake named after it.' Here are 28 yummy foods from around the UK. Can you match them to their birthplace on this map?

Bakewell tart

Banbury cake

Bath bun

Branston pickle

Brighton Blue cheese

Brown Windsor soup

Buxton blue cheese

Cheddar cheese

Chelsea bun

Chorley cake

Coventry god cakes

Devizes pie

Double Gloucester Cheese

Dover sole

Eccles cake

Eton mess

Everton mint

Kendal mint cake

Lincoln biscuit

Melton Mowbray pork pie

Oxford marmalade

Pontefract cake

Red Leicester cheese

Sandwich

Sturmer Pippin apple

Tewkesbury mustard

Worcestershire sauce (Worcester)

Yorkshire pudding (York)

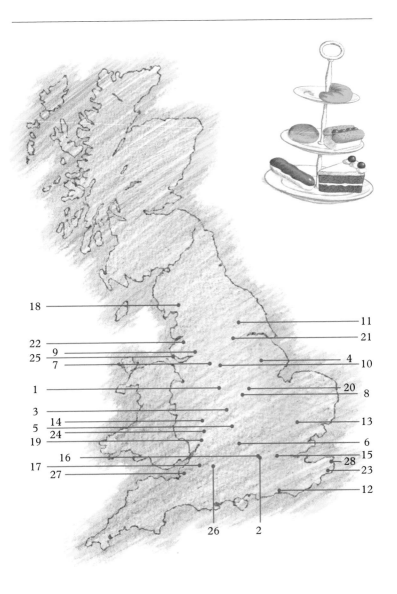

TEST No. 274723 • Time limit 5 minutes

MORRIS DANCING

Morris dancing is an English folk tradition that dates back to the Middle Ages when getting drunk, waving handkerchiefs and hitting each other with sticks was considered the height of sophistication at a time when people had few leisure pursuits, beyond self-flagellation and public floggings. Itinerant Morris dancers wore bells on their shins (and still do). Today, this acts as advance warning, but back then it announced their presence in each village, where they were met with jubilation because everyone could have the day off to let their bloody wheals crust over. How much do you know about Morris dancing?

1. Morris dancers must have body odour and a beard, even the women.

   a. true

   b. false

2. Which of the following items would you not associate with Morris dancing?

   a. deodorant

   b. beard trimmer

   c. having a partner

   d. all of the above

3. Which of the following instruments would commonly be used to accompany a Morris dance?

   a. tenor saxophone

   b. theremin

   c. fibre optic endoscope

   d. none of the above

4. What is the collective name for a set of Morris dancers performing a routine?

   a. set

   b. troupe

   c. clump

   d. flock

5. What is the name of the dancer who interacts with the audience?

   a. Geoff

   b. Gervaise

   c. Neville

   d. Jeremy

6. Which of the following is not someone associated with a troupe of Morris dancers?

a. Bagman

b. Squire

c. Zlatan Ibrahimović

d. Ragman

7. What name is given to an event where several Morris dancers perform to one another?

a. ponce off

b. yawnfest

c. ale

d. rap battle

8. Which of the following is not a Morris dance?

a. Laudanum Bunches

b. Bean Setting

c. Bean Flicking

d. Leap Frog

9. In ballet, what are you doing if you perform a 'pirouette'?

a. not Morris dancing

b. making a prank call

c. building a tree house

d. arranging a night out with friends

10. Apart from Geoff, how many Morris dancers can you name?

a. more than one

b. fewer than ten

c. none

d. forty-two

TEST No. 274724 • Time limit 3 minutes

JAMES BOND

The quintessentially British MI6 agent James Bond, licensed to pun, is arguably the most famous secret service operative in the world, invented by Ian Fleming, an Old Etonian and naval intelligence officer during WWII. Fleming named his protagonist after a boring American ornithologist and author of *Birds of the West Indies*. He wanted him 'to be an extremely dull, uninteresting man to whom things happened,' and he thought James Bond was 'the dullest name I ever heard.' His first novel, *Casino Royale,* published on 13th April 1953 was an instant hit. The first movie, *Dr. No,* was released in 1962, and as Sean Connery might say, 'The resht is hishtory.'

Can you match the correct cringeworthy punchlines to their set ups, to complete these ten dad jokes? Remember, these all appeared in the actual movies.

SET UPS

Live and Let Die: Kananga inflates like a balloon, flies up to the ceiling and explodes.	*Moonraker*: Hugo Drax: 'Why did you break up the encounter with my pet python?'	*Goldfinger*: Oddjob has just been fatally electrocuted. General: 'Where's your butler friend?'	*Die Another Day*: Madonna is teaching Bond fencing: 'I see you handle your weapon well.'	*Moonraker*: The Minister of Defence: 'My God, what's Bond doing?'
License to Kill: Felix Leiter gets fed to a shark. Attached to the body is a note that says:	*Thunderball*: Domino shoots Vargas in the back with a spear gun.	*A View to a Kill*: Jenny Flex: 'Yes, I love an early morning ride.'	*Tomorrow Never Dies*: Bond: 'I always enjoyed learning a new tongue.'	*GoldenEye*: Xenia Onatopp: 'You don't need the gun, Commander.'

PUNCHLINES

Bond: 'Well, I'm an early riser myself.'	Bond: 'Oh, he blew a fuse.'	Q: 'I think he's attempting re-entry, sir.'	Bond: 'Well, that depends on your definition of safe sex.'	Bond: 'I think he got the point.'
Bond: 'Oh, he always did have an inflated opinion of himself.'	Bond: 'I discovered it had a crush on me.'	Moneypenny: 'You always were a cunning linguist, James.'	Bond: 'I have been known to keep my tip up.'	'He disagreed with something that ate him.'

TEST No. 274725 • Time limit 5 minutes

AT THE BEACH

A day at a newly sovereign British beach is a love-hate venture, full of excitement and anticipation as well as multiple pitfalls. If blue skies happen to coincide with a bank holiday, or the weather pundits decide to mobilise the entire country using the trigger word 'heatwave', the roads and beaches immediately fill to capacity with dazed-looking families, mashed young thrill-seekers and hordes of pensioners in full winter attire.

1. Which two things does a Brit never forget to bring to the beach?

   a. one-man tent

   b. wind block

   c. football

   d. alcohol

2. What's the most appealing thing about a day at a British beach?

   a. spotting strawberry anemones and crabs among the rock pools

   b. walking barefoot in the dunes

   c. fossil hunting at low tide

   d. spelling out swear words in the damp sand

3. What is the ideal beach spot?

   a. close to the toilets

   b. close to the car park

   c. close to the chip shop

   d. all of the above

4. What's the worst thing about a day at a British beach?

   a. hobbling over pebbles

   b. freezing water

   c. litter and dog poo

   d. running out of Jägermeister

5. How often should you reapply sun block?

a. every hour

b. when my tattoos start itching and/or bleeding

c. as soon as my skin turns pink

d. I left it at home.

6. Thanks to pressure from the EU and a European Court of Justice ruling, in which year did British water companies finally stop dumping raw sewage into the sea?

a. 1972 (Surely we complied with EU targets as soon as we joined.)

b. 1979

c. 1984

d. 1998 (Yeah, you'd better believe it.)

7. Is it legal to drink alcohol on UK beaches?

a. yes

b. It's actually illegal, but police turn a blind eye so long as you aren't being a public nuisance.

c. Yes, although The Criminal Justice and Police act of 2001 gave councils the power to create 'designated public place orders' (DPPOs), where the police can confiscate your alcohol.

d. yes, except on Sundays

8. Is it legal to light bonfires on UK beaches?

a. In Scotland, you are advised to keep the fire 'wee, under control and supervised'.

b. You're not allowed to light any fires on a beach without the permission of the land owner, but the area between high and low tide actually belongs to the Crown.

c. National Trust beaches have a no fire policy.

d. Who cares? Those sweaty chicken thighs won't cook themselves.

9. What are you most likely to see on a day trip to a British beach?

a. beautiful white sand

b. scorching sun, hailstones and a rainbow

c. shallow turquoise water

d. stunning scenery

10. What are the first two things you do after spending a scorching Bank Holiday weekend on the beach?

a. share pictures of my sunburn and tan line fails on Instagram

b. apply natural yoghurt to my pink festering skin

c. throw a sickie on Tuesday

d. stock up on SPF50

TEST No. 274726 • Time limit 5 minutes

BUCKINGHAM PALACE

Buckingham Palace has been the official London residence of the UK's sovereign since 1837, and today it's the place from which HRH runs the whole shebang. British royalty is at least smart enough to have learned a few tricks since the French Revolution, and so despite the palace being used for swanky official business and elite receptions, a few of the 775 rooms are begrudgingly opened to visitors every summer. This nominal public access prevents the monarchy from ending up like Marie Antoinette, and also allows the royal family to trouser millions from the public purse.

It's a truly impressive building. When staunch royalists claim that the monarch attracts millions of tourists, in fact it's the turbo-charged townhouse at the end of the Mall that they come to gawp at, since the Queen is nowhere to be seen.

1. In the Middle Ages, a village stood within the site of the future palace grounds. What was it called?

a. Ewe Cross

b. Eye Cross

c. Brent Cross

d. King's Cross

2. Who was the first monarch to reside in Buckingham Palace?

a. Henry VIII

b. Queen Victoria

c. George III

d. George IV

3. How many bathrooms are there?

a. 183

b. 6

c. 78

d. 26

4. In 2016, Prime Minister David Cameron signed off on a 10-year schedule of maintenance work on the palace, funded by the British taxpayer, estimated to cost:

a. £125 million

b. £265 million

c. £369 million

d. £67 million

5. **Who is responsible for all flags flown from the palace?**

a. The Queen's Flag Sergeant

b. The Flag Flyer Pursuivant

c. Flaggy McFlagface

d. The Jolly Flagman

6. **During World War II, the palace suffered nine separate bombings, one of which destroyed the chapel, causing the Queen to famously declare:**

a. 'Hitler hat nur einen hoden.'

b. 'I'm glad we have been bombed. Now I can look the East End in the face.'

c. 'Doesn't Adolf know we're German?'

d. 'Oh goody, we could do with a new chapel.'

7. **Apart from the Queen and the Duke of Edinburgh, which royals still live with their parents in Buckingham Palace?**

a. Prince Charles and Camilla, Duchess of Cornwall

b. Prince Edward and Sophie, Countess of Essex

c. Prince Andrew, Duke of York

d. Anne, Princess Royal and Sir Timothy Laurence

8. **How often do they 'Change the Guard' at Buckingham Palace?**

a. more often than they change the sheets

b. four or five times a week, usually at 11:00am

c. whenever enough tourists have gathered outside

d. twice a day

9. **The state banquets and the conferring of knighthoods takes place in the largest room in the palace. What is it called?**

a. the ballroom

b. the snug

c. the front room

d. the big yellow room

10. **The palace employs two *what* to attend to the 350 *what*?**

a. public relations specialists to crisis manage the Duke of Edinburgh's yearly gaffes

b. horological conservators to maintain and wind up all the clocks

c. Michelin-starred chefs to feed the staff and residents

d. candle makers to stock the chandeliers

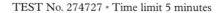

TEST No. 274727 • Time limit 5 minutes

OBSESSING ABOUT THE TRAFFIC

Everyone in Western Europe would agree that the volume of traffic on the roads is beyond a joke; Britain's drivers spend on average 32 hours a year in jams (although Belgium is the worst). Despite a rash of car-sharing schemes, bus lanes and all of us being encouraged to ditch our cars in favour of bikes or bring a sleeping bag to work, nothing can stop the exponential increase in road traffic. It's an annoyance, for sure, but if you're a middle-aged British male, you probably take your displeasure to extremes. Take this quiz to find out what hue of gridlock gammon you are.

1. **You're travelling very slowly bumper-to-bumper on a motorway. How do you react after the first half hour?**

   a. Stay patient: this can't last forever.

   b. I'm a bit miffed but everyone's in the same boat.

   c. Phone ahead to give my apologies for being late, then go with the flow.

   d. Work out how many hours my journey will take if I continue to travel at this speed, and keep whining and transmitting this data to my passengers every five minutes.

2. **The traffic jam becomes stationary. Some young guys start to play football on the hard shoulder. Do you join in?**

   a. Yeah, why not? They look like they're having fun.

   b. Good luck to them, but we could be moving again soon.

   c. Nah, they're young and carefree and I'm enjoying this Radio 4 play.

   d. Absolutely not. They are putting their lives and those of everyone else on the motorway in danger. I bet they're Polish. See, this is why I voted for Brexit.

3. How do you react when someone cuts you up?

a. It usually makes me giggle.

b. I feel sorry for someone who's in such a dangerous hurry.

c. I brake, then briefly honk my horn: safety first!

d. I beep the horn continuously for two minutes, then try to run them off the road whilst yelling obscenities.

4. Do you travel with any hardware in case someone disrespects you on the carriageway?

a. No, but I do have some jump leads which I'm happy to offer to those in need.

b. Just a bumper sticker that says 'If you can see read this, you may be a bit too close.'

c. I always keep a rolled-up copy of *Country Living*, which I wave about disapprovingly.

d. ball peen hammer, baseball bat, fifteen-inch bowie knife and a Glock G20

5. How do you feel about the 'baby on board' bumper sticker?

a. It's cute, they have a new arrival and feel both proud and safety conscious.

b. It's a bit twee but the protective message is still valid.

c. It does make me chuckle that people have to offer incentives to make other drivers slow down.

d. It drives me guano crazy. Why should they expect me to be extra careful just because their gametes are strapped in a few feet in front of me? I ALWAYS drive safely.

6. How do you feel about cyclists?

a. I'm grateful that they are reducing carbon emissions.

b. I admire their physical fitness and their bravery for taking their lives in their hands.

c. They don't bother me so long as they obey the Highway Code and don't skip traffic lights.

d. I loathe them clogging up my peripheral vision on their pointless circular journeys that begin at home and end back home, just to work up a sweat. If you're not making a necessary journey, keep off the road, you breathable-fabric-wearing freaks.

7. If you're stuck in traffic and you're alone in the car, what do you do?

a. I relish the silent solitude of my little steel bubble; I may be in a jam but my soul flies free.

b. I turn on the radio and enjoy some smooth classics.

c. I phone my other half to share the misery, and make dire predictions about when I'll be home.

d. I screech and bang on the steering wheel; with no one to judge me, my toddler ID goes into nuclear meltdown.

8. **Does your father-in-law always know a better route than the one you just took?**

a. I'm not married but I'm sure I'll enjoy soaking up his wisdom in the future, whoever he may be.

b. It's uncanny, and no matter where we are, his route always includes the A38.

c. All British fathers-in-law seem to know the A-road network better than that memory guy who counts cards down the Grosvenor every Friday night.

d. I swear to God, when we visit the in-laws, my feet have barely crossed the threshold and he's fetching the road atlas to show me three alternatives, because our traffic jam was on the local news.

9. **The best day for traffic is Monday. Does not knowing why make you seethe?**

a. Not at all, but I'm curious to know why. Is it because some of our industrious colleagues work flexi hours and choose Monday as their day off/at home?

b. Monday is also the day when my mobile phone is most likely to be nicked. So, the longer I'm in this traffic jam, the safer my phone is.

c. Is it because all the hungover skunk-addled wasters stay in bed on Mondays and reduce the commuter flow? I bet it is. This country is going to the dogs.

d. Livid. Too angry to even think about why, although it will definitely be something to do with the derivative hive mind of sweating humanity.

10. **What drives you the most crazy about traffic jams?**

a. Nothing really. It helps me to contemplate that we are all connected.

b. Not knowing what's causing the tailback. Some overhead info, even 'everyone's rubbernecking' would be useful.

c. Honestly, it makes me feel insignificant and lacking in control of my life.

d. Other people watching me pick my nose.

TEST No. 274728 • Time limit 2 minutes

HOW TO SPOT A REAL CORNISH PASTY

A Cornish pasty is made by placing an uncooked filling, typically meat and vegetables, on one half of a flat, shortcrust pastry circle, folding the pastry in half to form a D-shape and crimping the curved edge to seal before baking.

In 2011, the Cornish Pasty joined the likes of Champagne, Parma Ham and Jersey Royal potatoes as a protected origin product. It was awarded Protected Geographical Indication (PGI) designation, which covers products whose 'production, processing or preparation' takes places in a specific area.

Here are twelve pasties but only three of them are allowed to be called a Cornish Pasty. Can you spot them?

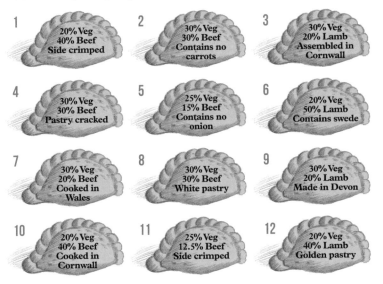

1
20% Veg
40% Beef
Side crimped

2
30% Veg
30% Beef
Contains no carrots

3
30% Veg
20% Lamb
Assembled in Cornwall

4
30% Veg
30% Beef
Pastry cracked

5
25% Veg
15% Beef
Contains no onion

6
20% Veg
50% Lamb
Contains swede

7
30% Veg
20% Beef
Cooked in Wales

8
30% Veg
30% Beef
White pastry

9
30% Veg
20% Lamb
Made in Devon

10
20% Veg
40% Beef
Cooked in Cornwall

11
25% Veg
12.5% Beef
Side crimped

12
20% Veg
40% Lamb
Golden pastry

TEST No. 274729 • Time limit 5 minutes

DOING DIY ON A BANK HOLIDAY WEEKEND

Britain is a nation of hazardous botchers; we may lack the skills, the tools and the patience to do a job, but that doesn't stop us from having a go. As A&E departments brace themselves for a spike in injuries, a sovereign bank holiday weekend is the perfect occasion to paper an alcove, give the bathroom a facelift or remodel some kerb appeal into your front garden. If those guys on *DIY SOS* can do it, what's to stop you tackling some overdue household tasks, especially when even the presenter looks like he just woke up in a hedge. The first step is to have a huge fry up, nip down to B&Q to pick up some random supplies and always stay safe while you work. It's time to refresh your safety knowledge …

1. **What's the first rule of Bank Holiday DIY?**

   a. Erm … buy some more dust sheets?

   b. Wear safety goggles and an old pair of flip flops.

   c. Good planning and preparation are two-thirds of the task.

   d. I'm just going to jump right in because this is a four-day job, really.

2. **How should you stay safe around power tools?**

   a. Wear baggy clothing – comfort is key.

   b. Keep them switched off when in use.

   c. Use a circuit breaker.

   d. Have a friend stand by with a wooden plank, ready to whack the tool from your rictus grip.

3. **You have a six-foot stepladder and need an eight-foot one. What do you do?**

   a. Swap flip flops for peep toe sandals.

   b. Buy a new ladder.

   c. Duct tape the ironing board to the top.

d. Rivet the ironing board to the bottom.

4. **When painting, or using materials that generate toxic fumes or dust, keep:**

   a. taking slow deep breaths

   b. all the doors and windows shut and tape over the cracks

   c. picking your nose to remove crusty residue

   d. the room well ventilated.

5. **Store tools in a safe place, out of the way of:**

   a. women

   b. children and pets

   c. cheapskate cadging neighbours

   d. rats and mice.

6. **Never perform electrical work when standing on what?**

   a. pointe

   b. someone else's shoulders

   c. an aluminium ladder

   d. the dock of the bay

7. **Complete the sentence. Never use _____ to fight fire in an electrical appliance.**

   a. fire

   b. milk

   c. water

   d. your feet

8. **When performing DIY, what's the best thing to follow?**

   a. your dreams

   b. instructions

   c. intuition

   d. Jesus

9. **Get into the habit of using *what*, whenever there's a chance of flying dust?**

   a. sunglasses

   b. vacuum cleaner

   c. protective wraparound goggles

   d. contact lenses

10. **When working on a ladder, always keep your hips *what*?**

    a. free from cellulite

    b. within the two vertical rails

    c. moisturised

    d. lower than your shoulders

Technical Challenge #5 • Time limit 5 minutes

MAKING THE PERFECT POT OF TEA

Whilst the custom of drinking tea dates back to the third millennium BC in China, the British came relatively late to the party. Tea drinking was made fashionable in England during the 1660s by King Charles II and his wife the Portuguese Infanta Catherine de Braganza – yet another pillar of Britishness that was erected by a foreigner.

The quintessential English tradition of 'afternoon tea' didn't appear until the mid-nineteenth century, but like most English customs, its provenance can be traced back to a single individual – in this instance, Anna, the seventh Duchess of Bedford – and the year 1840. There is scant historical evidence of any of the previous six duchesses suffering from the late afternoon munchies, but Anna complained of always feeling hungry around four o'clock. So she instructed her servants to bring her tea, bread and butter and cake to tide her over until the evening meal was served four hours later.

Naturally, the Victorian upper-classes quickly ruined this intimate snack hack by turning it into a dreary overblown social event, complete with long gowns, gloves and posh hats. In stuffy drawing rooms up and down the country, afternoon tea became a prime opportunity to showcase one's social graces.

YOUR FIVE-MINUTE CHALLENGE

You have five minutes to brew the perfect pot of tea that is so exquisite, the Queen herself would happily squeeze in a cup between all those gin and Dubonnets. Visualise her bringing the bone china to her lips, taking a sip and then smiling genially, rather than spraying a mouthful over the swagged curtains. Then look below to see if you followed the correct procedure. If not, humbly accept that you've been making tea wrong your entire life and promise yourself never to deviate from these instructions in the future.

HOW TO MAKE A PERFECT POT OF TEA

1. Empty the kettle, fill with fresh tap water and switch it on.

2. When the kettle is hot, pour some water into the empty teapot and swill it around to warm the pot, then tip it out.

3. Place one heaped teaspoon of loose leaf tea per cup into the warm empty teapot, plus one extra 'for the pot'.

4. Bring the water to the boil, and then immediately pour it into the teapot. Don't let the water boil for long, and do not re-boil the kettle if you missed it, otherwise the oxygen will escape from the water and make the tea taste flat.

5. Stir and then leave to brew for four minutes.

6. Pour into a bone china cup and then add the milk and sugar.

Key points:
- fresh water
- warm the teapot
- boil once
- bone china cup
- add milk and sugar to the tea, not vice-versa

A PENNY FOR THE GUY

'Penny for the Guy' is something you don't hear very often nowadays, even though everyone knows what it means. Kids used to make effigies of Guy Fawkes and then wheel them around the neighbourhood, begging pennies so they could save up for fireworks on Bonfire Night on 5th November, when the Guy would traditionally be burned on a big public bonfire.

Guy Fawkes planned the failed Gunpowder Plot of 1605, which was to blow up the House of Lords, kill King James I and restore the Catholic monarchy to the English throne. The plotters rented the basement underneath the House of Lords, where they stored all their gunpowder until Fawkes was captured there during the early hours of 5th November, following an anonymous tip-off.

Following several days of brutal torture, Fawkes confessed and named his seven fellow conspirators. On 31st January 1906 they were all hung, drawn and quartered (hanged almost to death, then while still conscious, had genitals and bowels removed, followed by beheading and body chopped into four pieces). Fawkes was the last to be executed, but somehow managed to jump from the scaffold with sufficient height or force to break his neck and die instantly, pain free. Winning!

YOUR THREE-MINUTE CHALLENGE

Can you help Guy Fawkes escape through the labyrinthine passages beneath the Old Palace of Westminster and reach the detonator within three minutes, before the palace guards discover his nefarious plot and chop off his nadgers?

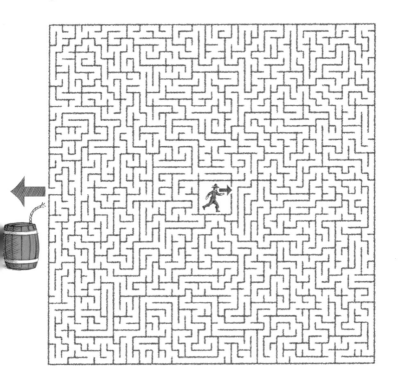

THE BOAT RACE

The Boat Race is an annual rowing contest between Oxford and Cambridge University Boat Clubs on the River Thames in London. Two crews – usually composed of the eight tallest and richest American postgraduate students from each university – go head-to-head to see who can row the 4.2-mile stretch of river the quickest, without puking up their breakfast. Over 250,000 braying middle-class Londoners line the route with picnic hampers and bubbly, and about eight million Brits turn on the telly to gawp at these rangy, overprivileged masochists, who all seem to be called Will, Benedict, Kelsey or Olivia.

1. **Members of both rowing crews are traditionally called 'blues'. Why?**

   a. After the race they all turn blue.

   b. They look like supersize extras from the film *Avatar*.

   c. The colours of Oxford and Cambridge are dark and light blue, respectively.

   d. The athletes remain celibate throughout their training.

2. **The course is 4 miles and 374 yards from Putney to Mortlake, but why does it follow an S shape?**

   a. because only the cox faces forward

   b. to fit more spectators along the route

   c. It makes it easier to row uphill.

   d. That's the way the Thames bends.

3. **Before the race, with what do the rowing clubs' presidents toss off to decide which side of the river to row on?**

   a. a 1829 gold sovereign

   b. their cox

   c. their cookies

   d. their gametes

4. **Situated 0.6km from the start of the race, the iconic 'Black Buoy' is the first landmark on the famous course. What colour is it?**

   a. black

   b. blue

c. black and blue

d. yellow

5. The Cambridge boat famously sank during the 1978 race. Oxford stayed afloat because they had fitted *what* to their boat?

a. futtock shrouds

b. splashboards

c. bilge rollocks

d. a cocktail cabinet

6. In 1984, the Cambridge boat famously sank (again) after colliding with what before the race had even started?

a. Clare Balding

b. barge

c. shopping trolley

d. iceberg

7. After the 1977 race, which legendary sports commentator amiably remarked live on air: 'Ah, isn't that nice, the wife of the Cambridge president is kissing the cox of the Oxford crew.'?

a. David Coleman

b. Frank Bough

c. Dickie Davies

d. Harry Carpenter

8. In 2012, three-quarters of the way into the race, a lone protester, Trenton Oldfield, obstructed the boats and the event had to be halted for half an hour. What was his beef?

a. Tory spending cuts

b. the erosion of civil liberties and a growing culture of elitism within British society

c. posh twats messing about in boats while urban poverty and inequality soared

d. all of the above

9. What do the rowing crews traditionally toss into the Thames at the end of the race?

a. Chelsea Pensioners

b. their cox

c. their cookies

d. their gametes

10. 'Boat race' is Cockney Rhyming Slang for *what*?

a. third base

b. face

c. pearl necklace

d. bouillabaisse

TEST No. 274731 • Time limit 3 minutes

BAKE OFF INNUENDO GENERATOR

Innuendo has been a staple of British humour ever since the Battle of Hastings when William the Conqueror famously pushed back his helmet and rode amongst his troops, and King Harold caught it in his eye. More recently, prime-time British television has kept the tradition alive, from Carry On films to its latest incarnation in cookery programmes. Before having your way with the innuendo generator, see if you can attribute these twenty quotes. Half are from *The Great British Bake Off* and the other half are from Nigella Lawson.

1. 'I adore the way it comes bulging up over the rims.'

2. 'Time to stop fiddling with Charlotte now.'

3. 'I'm going to try the old wiggling between two dangling things technique.'

4. 'These are my guiltless pleasures, they really are bulging.'

5. 'Oh no, you have some irregular-shaped balls.'

6. 'It's all in the wrist action.'

7. 'Ah, look at these gorgeous golden globules.'

8. 'If you would prefer something oozy and sticky to take up to bed with you, well, that's fine by me.'

9. 'Get those lady's fingers soggy!'

10. 'I love having an implement in each hand.'

11. 'I've never eaten a nun before.'

12. 'I'm already in position.'

13. 'The base is quite thick.'

14. 'Stand away from your hot baps!'

15. 'I feel I need an ungainly squirt.'

16. 'You want something quite rigid, but something that will taste good too.'

17. 'Typically I do it on the floor, because it gets so stiff.'

18. 'I'm not going in for full frontal guacamole.'

19. 'My empty vessels are ready to be loaded.'

20. 'I knew it would be easier by machine. But I just like to feel it.'

INNUENDO GENERATOR

Step 1: select a word based on the initial of your first name.

A – Soggy	N – Juicy
B – Fruity	O – Sticky
C – Mushy	P – Crumbly
D – Cheesy	Q – Beaten
E – Moist	R – Watery
F – Fluffy	S – Stiff
G – Salty	T – Smoky
H – Tender	U – Crunchy
I – Soft	V – Tossed
J – Creamy	W – Succulent
K – Buttery	X – Greasy
L – Rigid	Y – Flaky
M – Chewy	Z – Raw

Step 2: select a word based on the month of your birth.

January – Crumpet	July – Balls
February – Ring	August – Bottom
March – Nuts	September – Slice
April – Berries	October – Lady fingers
May – Crack	November – Muffin
June – Finish	December – Box

TEST No. 274732 • Time limit 5 minutes

WINSTON CHURCHILL

Winston Churchill was a game old bird whose protracted life was full of ups and downs. In his youth he was an impulsive – some would say feckless – character full of overweening hubris and derring-do. At school he won no plaudits, but went on to scoop the Nobel Prize for Literature aged 79, the icing on the cake after his earlier achievement of slam dunking WWII.

The airbrushed version of him we've canonised is the elderly gammon-faced bulldog, who replaced a youthful stutter and terror of public speaking with a transcendent knack of tapping into the mood of a nation, plus a more up-market speech impediment called a rhotacism – colloquially known as buggering up the 'r's.

But how much do you know about the chequered existence of the man considered by many to be the greatest Briton who ever lived?

1. Winston Leonard Spencer-Churchill was born in 1874 at his grandfather's famous seat. What was it called?

a. bathtub chair from *Breakfast at Tiffany's*

b. Oprah's couch

c. Blenheim Palace

d. bench from *Forrest Gump*

2. Churchill enrolled at Sandhurst as an officer cadet in September 1893. How many times did he fail the entrance exam?

a. twice

b. three times

c. five times

d. seven times

3. Employed as a war reporter, he spent his 21st birthday in Cuba, acquiring which two vices?

a. mojitos and psychotropics

b. Spanish omelettes and salsa

c. siestas and Havana cigars

d. fried plantains and rum

4. He was captured in Sount Africa during The Boer War. How did he escape?

a. jumped over a barbed wire fence on a motorbike

b. dug a hole through his prison wall, hidden by a poster of Raquel Welch

c. jumped on a passing train and hid among sacks

d. built a glider out of toilet roll tubes

5. **Churchill delivered his first speech in Parliament in 1901. He overcame his lisp with meticulous preparation. After getting the chokes in the House of Commons in 1904, he always used *what* thereafter?**

a. detailed notes

b. teleprompter

c. St John's wort

d. stress balls

6. **In 1908, he became the youngest *what* since 1866?**

a. member of The 1922 Committee

b. prime minister

c. cabinet minister

d. chain smoker

7. **In 1911, he became *what*, spearheading rapid growth in the naval arms race with Germany?**

a. anti-German

b. a non-executive director of BAE Systems

c. a Freemason

d. First Lord of the Admiralty

8. **In the 1924 General Election, Churchill won the Epping seat as *what*?**

a. Labour

b. Conservative

c. Liberal

d. Independent Constitutionalist anti-Socialist

9. **After losing his seat in 1929, he became increasingly marginalised during the early thirties and no one listened to his warnings about which prominent Nazi?**

a. Diana Mitford

b. Edward VIII

c. Lord Rothermere

d. Adolf Hitler

10. **In January 1955, aged 80, he failed to persuade his cabinet to agree to use which slogan to restrict West Indian immigration into Britain?**

a. Britain is Full

b. Keep England White

c. You Will Not Replace Us

d. Blood and Soil

Technical Challenge #7 • Time limit 5 minutes

HOW MUCH DUNKIRK SPIRIT DO YOU HAVE?

The Dunkirk evacuation, aka Operation Dynamo, remains one of the most emotive and famous events of the Second World War and was called a 'miracle of deliverance' by Winston Churchill, even though it was essentially a mass retreat of 338,226 British and other Allied forces who were trapped on the beaches of Northern France and were a sitting target for the Germans, who had surprised everyone by launching a high-risk attack through the forest of the Ardennes (after which Hitler declared himself to be a military genius). From 26th May to 4th June 1940, a hastily assembled fleet of over 800 boats, big and small, rescued 338,226 soldiers from the beaches. Smaller ships were essential to ferry the men from the shore to the larger ships; the smallest of these was the Tamzine, an 18-foot fishing boat.

The winners write the history books, so Dunkirk is viewed today as a great victory, even though at the time it was like Tim Henman, trailing by two sets in a Wimbledon semi-final, fighting to stay in the game by winning a third-set tie-breaker. The difference is that whereas Timbo would typically balls up the fifth set and lose the match, the Allied Forces actually managed to win the war, so Dunkirk has become synonymous with British pluck and heroism, rather than a humiliating early indicator of an inevitable trouncing. 'Dunkirk Spirit' is an attitude of being very strong in a difficult situation and refusing to accept defeat.

YOUR FIVE-MINUTE CHALLENGE

Think of a time in your life when you suffered a humiliating defeat. Scribble yourself a letter of self-serving bloviating propaganda that transforms this terrible moment into a shining beacon of glorious triumph. Some people actually do this routinely; they're called sociopaths and many of them are currently running the world. Feels good doesn't it? Award yourself extra points for hyperbole and blatant lies.

TEST No. 274733 • Time limit 3 minutes

RUDE PLACE NAMES

Although the Brits love their double-entendres (see page 112) they like nothing better than an in-yer-face bit of smut; and where better to get satisfaction than rude place names? Thanks to the richness of the English language, the UK can boast some of the filthiest places in the world. Listed below are thirty street signs with outrageous names. Half of them *actually exist*. See if you can pick them out.

Beaver Close, Surrey	Lickfold, West Sussex
Bell End, Worcestershire	Lickham Bottom, Devon
Boggy Bottom, Hertfordshire	Minge Lane, Worcestershire
Bonar Bridge, Scotland	Nob End, South Lancashire
Brown Willy, Cornwall	North Piddle, Worcestershire
Cheese Bottom, South Yorkshire	Rimswell, East Riding of Yorkshire
Cockermouth, Cumbria	Scratchy Bottom, Dorset
Crotch Crescent, Oxfordshire	Shitterton, Dorset
Cumming Court, Gloucestershire	Slack Bottom, West Yorkshire
Fanny Barks, Durham	Slag Lane, Merseyside
Fine Bush Lane, Greater London	Sluts Hole Lane, Norfolk
Fingringhoe, Essex	Spanker Lane, Derbyshire
Friars Entry, Oxfordshire	Tickle Cock Bridge, West Yorkshire
Galloping Bottom, Somerset	Twatt, Orkney
Hornyold Road, Worcestershire	Wetwang, Yorkshire

ANSWERS

FISH AND CHIPS p.8

1. c
2. d
3. d
4. a, b, d
5. d
6. a
7. b
8. d
9. c
10. d

THE RULES OF CRICKET p.11

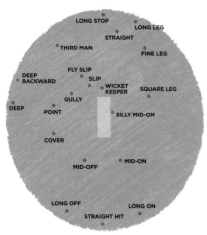

LONG STOP
LONG LEG
STRAIGHT
THIRD MAN
FINE LEG
FLY SLIP
DEEP BACKWARD
SLIP
WICKET KEEPER
SQUARE LEG
GULLY
DEEP
POINT
SILLY MID-ON
COVER
MID-ON
MID-OFF
LONG OFF
LONG ON
STRAIGHT HIT

THE SUNDAY ROAST p.14

```
T R I M M I N G S E D I S P O T U R K E Y H F
W A E I V V L K R O P W W V E G E T A B L E S
I U C P V G N I D D U P E R I H S K R O Y C M
S U G Y H K Q D Q L D K D V K I N T G Y L R U
H I P Y G T S I O M B B E P A R S N I P J I S
B J U I C E S G S H M A Q Y V I I M Z Y D S T
O R I L O C C O R B O K C O R V F Y M A H P A
N R E Y C Z Q N X Y A I C A R R O T V U W L R
E O W A B A X S K Z M N Y A S T U F F I N G D
Y S N N S E B S N G K G C L E G H W F B B X F
C E S T P T E B B U T T E R N U T S Q U A S H
H M R E X E P F A O P R R Q E X G H Y O V B S
I A E N J V A H U G U A S E O T A T O P O H C
C R T D C F E S B D E Y L Q W R I B Y I M R R
K Y S E J R F O B Y V A R G L O P D L F S O A
E X A R B J S I L V E R S I D E L E W J E A C
N G O S P R I N G G R E E N S G D F W M G S K
P A R S O N S N O S E L J D T S N Z I T A T L
P I G S I N B L A N K E T S N O K V M L S E I
S P R O U T S G U R B M A L C A M E J Y U D N
S X M C I L R A G K D P W A E I L A E Q A A G
H O R S E R A D I S H B B I N C C O R L S S C
S A G E A N D O N I O N M T A X X B C O T G R
```

LAST NIGHT OF THE PROMS p.16

1. b
2. d
3. a
4. a
5. a, b, c, d

DRIVING IN BRITAIN p.18

Beware Nazi road painters

Man struggling with umbrella

Prostate exam

Stunt motorcyclists

Red cars keep to the left

Alien abductions

Dumb lorry drivers

Cut-and-shut job

Sandy camel toe

Tailgating BMW drivers

Beeyooobs

Beware rickets!

Ferry service cancelled

Giant electronic piano mat

No admission without a tie

Ip Man

Suitable for home freezing

Juggling workshop

Road buffering ahead

Crucifixion

THE FULL ENGLISH
BREAKFAST p.20
bacon = 6g
sausage = 15g
fried egg = 5g

NATIONAL STEPHENS p.22
1. b (Oscar Wilde)
2. b (Brian Cox)
3. a (Woody Allen)
4. a (Morrissey)
5. a (Ken Loach)
6. c (Ricky Gervais)
7. c (Ronnie O'Sullivan)
8. a (Jimmy White)
9. b (Tom Jones)
10. d (Roy Keane)

TALKING ABOUT THE
WEATHER p.25
1. d

2. b
3. b
4. a
5. c
6. d
7. b
8. d
9. a, b
10. d

THE NHS p.28

THE WORLD CUP WORD
LADDER p.29
Blindly Optimistic → Deluded →
Wary → Angry → Mournful →
Suicidal

THE RULES OF BRITISH
QUEUING p.30
1. d
2. a1, b2, d3, c4

3. d
4. c
5. d
6. b, c, d
7. d
8. a, (d in London)
9. c
10. d

WALES p.34
1. d
2. b
3. d
4. b
5. d
6. c, d
7. d
8. a
9. a
10. d
11. a
12. d
13.d
14. b
15. a, b, d

BEING OVERLY POLITE p.37
All answers are 'sorry'.

PANTOMIME p.38
1. Licking the nuts, where's the soap, in my box, wax off <innuendo>
2. Goose, Trott, Twankey, Sara the Cook <Dames>
3. 'He's behind you!', 'Oh yes she is!', 'Oh no he isn't!', 'Shut up you annoying twat!' <audience participation>
4. Puss, ring, Dick, Jack <can't remember why>

SCOTLAND p.39
1. c	9. a (true)
2. b	10. b
3. c	11. a
4. c	12. d
5. d	13. d
6. a	14. d
7. b	15. b
8. c	

ALL-YOU-CAN-EAT BUFFET p.42

```
T G A S O M A S H E L U O B B A T O H J C S
O P P R S A R D A M G G E H C T O C S G J S
R A M E A T B A L L I K A Y N A P P E T E J
T K S T D M U O A B L Z M S A A G K U N U G
I O Q R R N I Q R Z Z C F Z C R S K C X B O
L R Q U U G P M U I O Y R R U C K G V M W Y
L A A F M R O O P R W A N E L B A T U M M N
A A S K S A O U M B W Y G S A M L O D F A R
C M K N T V B S E F A J I T A S N V R I E O
Y R C A I Y U S T P U Y C S L P U V I S R G
R O I R C T R A P R U S H P L N G S B H C A
E K T F K I G K F A Y U I A O Z G C S A E N
V G S T J K E A E W D S C G R A E A I N C J
R A B E W K R G B N O H K H G L T L R D I O
A L A O B A P A H T D I E E N L S L O C Y S
C A R F H A S L I Y I D N T I E T O O H X H
D S C F S M B R V L A W B T R A D P D I S L
G A T W A P R E N Y B H A I P P J S N P G C
Q M M T G U I K K T E S L F S V P R A S N X
G Y I Q B D Q H K S T S L E S S U M T C I I
Y O H C A N P X C A E M S Q U I C H E T W Q
Z E C H I C K E N P S N W T X E G A S U A S
```

WATCHING FOOTBALL DOWN THE PUB p.44

BIG BEN p.45

17: Big bell, A, B, C, D, AB, AC, AD, BC, BD, CD, ABC, ABD, ACD, BCD, ABCD, Big bell

THE BEATLES p.46

1. a	6. a
2. d	7. b
3. c	8. b
4. b	9. b
5. b	10. d

CHEESE ROLLING p.48

THE GRAND NATIONAL p.49

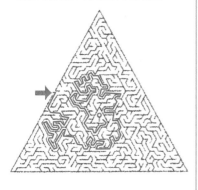

THE GRAND NATIONAL p.50

```
C NUMBERSIXVALVERDEGNIPPIHW
Z C B S S P I I WINNINGPOST E I R E M D N
Y J R N Z D NTIPPERARYTIM X L K C Q S M
A C P E C J I N H H I S SGGIRBALLAB C L T
O O G U U Y A N J T FAVOURITE P G X F A K Z
E E S R O H E CARASNEERCSNEER G U K Q
K O YEMOMNOM U E S A H CELPEET S G F M
D O N T P U S H I T N I DFATALITIES H E F
CANALTURNER O C N E S A R O R U A R O N R
E E R U L I A FTRAEHLETHAL C H Y S O C A
A T H P W BROKENANKLETHECHAIRE C
N N R H F O H B X I C S UOREGNADS Q F T S T
O U H O G O E E THOROUGHBRED A H R W K U
I H C T C G IGNA E D W S A H A D P O R COBDR
T L A O F Q Z NAEIPAAVIOGCKMRNNKE
CALFLGF CANLSA F L K A Y P A U I T Z T H
RNAIUNTOVVRLACBECHERSBROOK
AOGNTOOMZGOAYNIMTLXNYRUYZD
FIEITLOPAZGNCGAD V S O U E ENEMA
NTRSERHLSFBSVLDHNMDGLVNKUL
IAGHRUSYAYOVNFSRTAPTXLECRU
X N M I V F P O H G S Q L V H T OUHOFIRODE
E G V W A A G REERTNIA Z G L E H Q S T J E U
F STEWARDSENQUIRYFALSESTART
L MURDERI U T I J K BETTING D I N R O Y
B Z L Q L N SEGNOLLOCENUTPEN U P X F
```

LAWNS p.52

1. b, c	6. a, b
2. b, c	7. b, d
3. a	8. b, d
4. d	9. a, b
5. a, c	10. b, c

GOING FOR A NICE WALK p.55

THE ROYAL FAMILY p.58

1. a, b, c, d
2. a
3. b
4. b
5. d
6. a
7. d
8. d
9. c
10. c

SOAP OPERAS p.60

SOAP OPERAS p.62

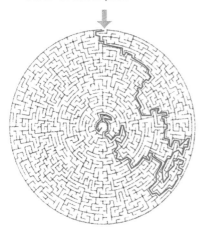

ENGLAND p.63

1. b
2. a, b, c, d
3. d
4. d
5. a, b, c, d
6. England rugby shirt, Manchester United strip, Beefeater, Morris Dancer
7. d
8. d
9. c
10. a (the other three are steamed)
11. a, b, c, d
12. b (The Tudor Rose)
13. a
14. 1b, 2d, 3c, 4a
15. 1b, 2c, 3d, 4a

PIGEON FANCYING p.66

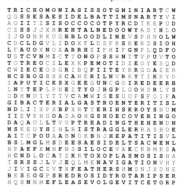

WIMBLEDON p.68

Across

2. John Lloyd
4. Singles final

8. Tim Henman
9. Sue Barker
10. Tim Henman
11. Rafael Nadal
12. Ginger
13. Tim Henman
Down
1. Cliff Richard
3. Tim Henman
5. Grunt
6. Tim Henman
7. Tim Henman
11. Royal box
13. Tim Henman

WIMBLEDON p.70
1. Serena Williams, Maria Sharapova, Victoria Azarenka, Elena Baltacha <Female grunters>
2. Rafael Nadal, Novak Djokovic, David Ferrer, Gustavo Kuerten <Male grunters>
3. When changing ends, players didn't use chairs until 1974, when 90 second commercial breaks were introduced.
4. Yellow balls were introduced in 1986; they are made by Slazenger and are kept at a temperature of 20°C.

NORTHERN IRELAND p.71
1. a
2. a, d
3. a
4. d
5. c

6. b
7. a
8. c
9. a
10. a
11. a
12. a
13. a, b, c, d
14. b
15. b, c

FOR THE LOVE OF RADIO 4 p.74
Across
2. *Front Row*
6. *The Archers*
7. Melvyn Bragg
8. *The Now Show*
9. Kate Adie
11. *Ramblings*
13. *Gardeners' Question Time*
14. Forty-five
Down
1. *You and Yours*
3. *Today Programme*
4. Shipping Forecast
5. Jonathan
8. *The News Quiz*
10. *Saturday Live*
12. Jones

STONEHENGE p.80
1. a, b	6. b
2. c	7. a, c
3. c	8. b
4. d	9. a, c
5. a	10. b

CASUAL AND INSTITUTIONAL PREJUDICE p.82

Across

3. Aidan Burley
6. Nigel Farage
8. Boris Johnson
10. Robert Fraser
12. Rosemary Carroll
13. Alan Mellins
14. Boris Johnson
15. Boris Johnson

Down

1. Nadine Dorries
2. Boris Johnson
4. Nigel Farage
5. Oliver Letwin
7. Peter Hobbins
9. Boris Johnson
11. Bob Frost

WATCHING CRICKET p.84

```
U N E X C I T I N G S N I C K O M E T E R B Q
G L O V E W E A R I S O M E T H G I L D A B S
F U L L T O S S R L L S G N I N N I O X L U I
U X E J E F C L A S S I M S I D Y P Y O M V W
Y O B R R A C A Z J H I K Q X G X R I P K Q E
L B O E T J S A K C D J D Y H E A T I E I E L
B Y W T S W S H U K E G G H L D C R B N N L H
B A L T U H I O E G X Z E K N G E U N E S B T
O W E U L M N C X S H L T U G K O W K R W A R
D N D C K V I I K F M T O H B T P O K O I N O
Y I R Y C R E M A E B B B B A I L S G T N I W
L N L S A W G N T R T A A E G V T Y S H G M K
B F A I L D B N X I X T H T H Z X D P G E R C
B I C A E P O A C B S H M X A I U P M U R E U
I E G D S J D D X M T O Y A T M N R U A B T D
D L N L A A Y T A E F W X R I O P D T C Q N N
T D I O E F L N R Y C Z O E U D F E S A M I T
E R R I R F I L N I X A B E D T E I R P X K Z
D E O G C A N U V I S T I C K Y N N E I S W R
I K B A L E E N Q E B E F W A W J E H L N A E
O R K C U D D C S U O N O T O N O M C N D G V
U O F P N I G H T W A T C H M A N Y T H F E O
S Y U L A N O I T A N R E T N I Y A D E N O R
```

GOING FOR A CURRY p.86

CHEERING THE UNDERDOG p.87

Row 1. Eric 'The Eel' Moussambani; Susan Boyle; Billy Elliot; *Zulu*: (Battle of Rorke's Drift)

Row 2. Jamaican Bobsleigh team; Frodo Baggins; Charlie Bucket; Goran Ivanišević

Row 3. Eddie the Eagle; Oliver Twist; Rocky Balboa; Leicester City

CREAM TEAS p.88

Devonshire cream tea: scone, cream jam

Cornish cream tea: scone, jam, cream

NAMING CAKES AFTER NORTHERN TOWNS p.90

1. Branston Pickle

2. Brown Windsor Soup
3. Coventry God Cakes
4. Lincoln Biscuit
5. Banbury Cake
6. Oxford Marmalade
7. Buxton Blue Cheese
8. Red Leicester Cheese
9. Eccles Cake
10. Bakewell Tart
11. Yorkshire Pudding (York)
12. Brighton Blue Cheese
13. Sturmer Pippin Apple
14. Worcestershire Sauce (Worcester)
15. Chelsea Bun
16. Eton Mess
17. Bath Bun
18. Kendal Mint Cake
19. Double Gloucester Cheese
20. Melton Mowbray Pork Pie
21. Pontefract Cake
22. Chorley Cake
23. Dover Sole
24. Tewkesbury Mustard
25. Everton Mint
26. Devizes Pie
27. Cheddar Cheese
28. Sandwich

MORRIS DANCING p.92

1. a
2. d
3. d
4. a
5. a
6. c
7. c
8. c
9. a
10. b

JAMES BOND p.94

Live and Let Die: Kananga inflates like a balloon, flies up to the ceiling and explodes.
Bond: 'Oh, he always did have an inflated opinion of himself.'

Moonraker: Hugo Drax: 'Why did you break up the encounter with my pet python?'
Bond: 'I discovered it had a crush on me.'

Goldfinger: Oddjob has just been fatally electrocuted. General: 'Where's your butler friend?'
Bond: 'Oh, he blew a fuse.'

Die Another Day: Madonna is teaching Bond fencing: 'I see you handle your weapon well.'
Bond: 'I have been known to keep my tip up.'

Moonraker: The Minister of Defence: 'My God, what's Bond doing?'
Q: 'I think he's attempting re-entry, sir.'

License to Kill: Felix Leiter gets fed to a shark. Attached to the body is a note that says:
'He disagreed with something that ate him.'

Thunderball: Domino shoots Vargas in the back with a spear gun.
Bond: 'I think he got the point.'

A View to a Kill: Jenny Flex, 'Yes, I love an early morning ride.'
Bond: 'Well, I'm an early riser myself.'

Tomorrow Never Dies: Bond: 'I always enjoyed learning a new tongue.'
Moneypenny: 'You always were a cunning linguist, James.'

GoldenEye: Xenia Onatopp: 'You don't need the gun, Commander.'
Bond: 'Well, that depends on your definition of safe sex.'

AT THE BEACH p.96
1. c, d
2. d
3. d
4. d
5. b
6. d
7. c
8. d
9. b
10. a, c

BUCKINGHAM PALACE p.98
1. b
2. b
3. c
4. c
5. a
6. b
7. b, c
8. a, b
9. a
10. b

OBSESSING ABOUT THE TRAFFIC p.100
Mostly As: you will live long and prosper. May your blood pressure always remain within a healthy range.
Mostly Ds: you are cruising for an embolism – have you thought of quitting your job and living on an Ashram?
Anywhere in-between means you're pretty standard (although still a delightful and unique individual).

HOW TO SPOT A REAL CORNISH PASTY p.103
A Cornish Pasty must contain at least 12.5% diced or minced beef and 25% vegetable content (potato, onion, swede NOT turnip) and be assembled in Cornwall. However, it can be baked outside of the designated production area. It must be side-crimped (not top-crimped) along the round side (not all the way round). The cooked pastry must be golden and not cracked. So the only ones that can be Cornish Pasties (so long as they meet the other criteria) are numbers 2, 7 and 11.

DOING DIY ON A BANK HOLIDAY WEEKEND p.104
1. c
2. c
3. b
4. d

5. b
6. c
7. a, b, c, d
8. b
9. c
10. b, d

A PENNY FOR THE GUY p.108

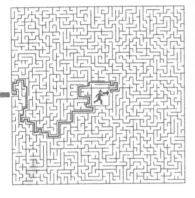

THE BOAT RACE p.110

1. c
2. d
3. a
4. d
5. b
6. b
7. d
8. d
9. b
10. b

BAKE OFF INNUENDO GENERATOR p.112

Nigella: 1, 4, 7, 8, 10, 12, 13, 15, 18, 19

The Great British Bake Off: 2, 3, 5, 6, 9, 11, 14, 16, 17, 20

WINSTON CHURCHILL p.114

1. c
2. a
3. c
4. c
5. a
6. c
7. d
8. d
9. d
10. b

RUDE PLACE NAMES p.117

Give up? The joke's on you because they are ALL real.

An Hachette UK Company
www.hachette.co.uk

First published in Great Britain in 2018 by Hamlyn, an imprint of
Octopus Publishing Group Ltd
Carmelite House
50 Victoria Embankment
London EC4Y 0DZ
www.octopusbooks.co.uk

Design and Layout Copyright © Octopus Publishing Group Limited 2018
Text Copyright © SJG Gift Publishing 2018

Text by Michael Powell
Cover Design by Milestone Creative
Ink drawings by Victor McLindon

ISBN 978-0-600-63573-4

A CIP catalogue record for this book is available from the British Library.

Printed and bound in the Czech Republic

10 9 8 7 6 5 4 3 2 1

Publishing Director: Trevor Davies
Senior Production Manager: Peter Hunt